Selections From
Julius Caesar's
Gallic War

Edited with Introductions,
Vocabularies and Notes

John C. Sang

Crossroads School for Arts and Sciences

UNIVERSITY
PRESS OF
AMERICA

Lanham • New York • London

Copyright © 1991 by
University Press of America®, Inc.
4501 Forbes Boulevard, Suite 200
Lanham, Maryland 20706

3 Henrietta Street
London WC2E 8LU England

Library of Congress Cataloging-in-Publication Data

Sang, John ., 1950-
Selections from Julius Caesar's Gallic War / edited with
introduction, vocabularies, and notes by John C. Sang.
p.   cm.
Selections in Latin, with notes and commentary in English.
Includes bibliographical references.
1. Latin language—Readers.   2. Gaul—History—Gallic Wars,
58-51 B.C.   I. Caesar, Julius. De bello Gallico. 1991.   II. Title.
PA2095.S263   1991
478.6'421—dc20   90–49864 CIP

ISBN 0–8191–8043–2 (pbk.: alk. paper)

For Rose and Andreas

ACKNOWLEDGEMENTS

p.4 Map of Gaul reprinted by permission of George Philip Limited, London.

p.29 Reconstruction of *corvus* from *The Ancient Mariners* by Lionel Casson. Copyright (c) 1959 Lionel Casson. Reprinted with permission of Macmillan Publishing Company.

p.33 Drawings of ships from *Denkmaeler des klassischen Altertums zur Erlaeuterung des Lebens der Griechen und Roemer in Religion, Kunst und Sitte* edited by August Baumeister. R. Oldenbourg. Munich and Leipzig 1885-1888.

p.37 Plan of Caesar's bridge from *Caesar's Commentaries on the Gallic War* by A. Harkness and C. Forbes. American Book Company. New York, Cincinnati, Chicago 1901.

p.41 Drawing of Caesar's bridge from *The Battle for Gaul* translated by Anne and Peter Wiseman. Illustrated by Barry Cunliffe. Translation copyright (c) 1980 by Anne Wiseman. Illustrations copyright (c) 1980 by Barry Cunliffe. Reproduced by permission of David R. Godine, Publisher.

p.44 Picture of model of Celtic chariot reproduced by permission of the National Museum of Wales, Cardiff.

p.50 Map of Caesar's geography of Britain from A.T. Walker, *Caesar's Gallic War*. Scott, Foresman and Company. Chicago 1907.

p.62 Diagram of structure of Celtic society from *The Battle for Gaul* translated by Anne and Peter Wiseman. Illustrated by Barry Cunliffe. Translation copyright (c) 1980 by Anne Wiseman. Illustrations copyright (c) 1980 by Barry Cunliffe. Reproduced by permission of David R. Godine, Publisher.

p.71 Reconstruction of siege-works at Alesia from *Histoire de Jules Cesar* by Napoleon III.

pp.75ff. Translation from *The Conquest of Gaul* translated by S.A. Handford, revised by Jane F. Gardner (Penguin Classics, Revised Edition, 1982), copyright (c) the Estate of S.A. Handford, 1951, revisions copyright (c) Jane F. Gardner, 1982. Reproduced by permission of Penguin Books Ltd., Harmondsworth, Middlesex, England.

Latin text reprinted from the Oxford Classical Texts edition of *Caesar: Commentarii I (Gallic War)* edited by R.L.A. du Pontet (1900) by permission of Oxford University Press.

TABLE OF CONTENTS

PREFACE

The purpose of this book is to make available a selection from Caesar's *Commentaries* on the Gallic War that does not focus, as is usually the case, on one or at most two books, but rather includes passages from Books I through VII; Book VIII has not been included since it was not written by Caesar but by Aulus Hirtius.

I hope that through the passages and the English prefaces that introduce them readers will acquire a broader knowledge of Caesar's campaigns in Gaul than would be acquired from a more narrowly focussed selection. I also hope that this selection will show that there is more to Caesar's *Commentaries* than the accounts of military maneuvers and battles that doubtless earned him among generations of schoolchildren a reputation for dullness. I am thinking especially of his descriptions of the peoples with whom he came into contact: the Britons, Gauls and Germans.

For each passage there is an accompanying vocabulary. If I have erred on the side of generosity with words given, it is because I would like to facilitate the reading of the text for students who are tackling the *Gallic War* as one of the first examples of original Latin that they read, i.e. students of Intermediate Latin in college, or Latin II and beyond in high school. It should be noted, however, that words that ought to be known by the end of the first two years of Latin are only given once in the word lists, at their first occurrence, at which time they are marked with an asterisk. It is assumed that instructors will require their students to memorize these words. Should they not be remembered in a subsequent passage they can be looked up in an alphabetical list of these words in an appendix at the end of the book. I have been helped in decisions about the vocabulary by John K. Colby's *Latin Word Lists*.

The endnotes for the General Introduction and for the prefaces to the Latin passages contain references to both primary and secondary sources. More mature students, who wish to read further, are empowered by these to do so.

The text I have used is that established by R. du Pontet (*Scriptorum Classicorum Bibliotheca Oxoniensis*) and published in 1900. I have, however, printed third declension accusative plurals in *-is* with *-es*, and on one occasion, noted beneath the text, I have followed other editors.

There are several people to whom I am greatly indebted and whom I thank very sincerely for their help and support: the members of the sabbatical committee at Crossroads School for giving me a one-semester sabbatical during which I completed this project; the headmaster, Paul Cummins, for his advocacy of both Latin and Greek at Crossroads; my colleagues at Crossroads, Jeff Cooper, Annetta Kapon and Gabriel Firth, who helped me by reading and commenting on parts of the manuscript; Michael Moore, without whose extraordinarily generous assistance in computer matters I would have had considerable difficulty in bringing this project to its conclusion. The person to whom I owe the greatest debt of all is included in the dedication.

J.C.S.

INTRODUCTION

Caesar's *Commentarii* and *Commentarius* as a literary form[1]

The surviving writings of Julius Caesar that we possess were called *C. Iuli Caesaris commentarii rerum gestarum*: 'Julius Caesar's commentaries on his achievements'. These include seven books on the Gallic War, covering the years 58 to 52 B.C., and three on the Civil War. The eighth book of the Gallic War was not written by Caesar but by his friend Aulus Hirtius, who had been one of his officers.

The *Commentaries* are to be distinguished from Caesar's despatches (*litterae*) which he sent from time to time to the Senate in Rome. Caesar refers to these on several occasions, and it is likely that he made use of them in writing the *Commentaries*.[2]

Caesar's account of the conquest of Gaul is unique in Roman historical writing, providing as it does "the only contemporary narrative of a major Roman imperialist war, and that by its principal agent".[3] Some modern scholars have called into question the accuracy of this account while others, who allow that no-one can achieve complete impartiality, point out how difficult it would have been for him to deceive the well-informed upper class readership to whom the *Commentaries* were directed.[4] The conclusion of H.H. Scullard, reached after careful weighing of the arguments of both sides, is judicious and worth repeating: "His work has stood up well to critical attacks and its essential trustworthiness is beyond question".[5]

The Commentary as a literary form was the culmination of a long process of development. The word *commentarius* corresponds to the Greek word *hypomnema* ('memoir'). This term might be applied to official despatches, minutes, administrative reports, private papers or diaries. Such writings were not, initially, intended for publication. They were a narrative statement of facts for purposes of record-keeping or aiding the memory.

Roman statesmen developed the Commentary into a published factual account of their achievements. This development, exemplified above all by Caesar's *commentarii*, had occurred before Caesar's time. We know, for example, of memoirs of the dictator Sulla.

The Romans made a distinction between *commentarius* and *historia*. Full History was a highly polished literary work of art for which a

Commentary might serve as a basis. Cicero said that Caesar wrote his *Commentarii* "because he wanted others, who might want to write history, to have source material to hand".[6] His further remarks in connection with the *Commentaries* that Caesar "frightened off sensible men from writing" and that "nothing in history is more pleasing than unaffected and lucid brevity" show that in capable hands *commentarius* could approximate closely to *historia*.[7] Cicero believed, in effect, that "Caesar's *Commentaries* challenged *historia* on its own ground with comparable, if not identical, qualities".[8]

The time of composition and publication of Caesar's *Commentarii*[9]

It cannot be stated with certainty either when Caesar composed or published his *Commentaries* on the Gallic War. According to one school of thought he wrote all seven books at one time, which would have been after his suppression of the great rebellion of 52 B.C., while according to another he wrote them at intervals, probably in the winters following each campaign in Gaul.

We shall never be able to settle this dispute with finality, but there are some factors that make intermittent composition more likely. For one, no book contains an undisputed forward reference to a later book. If Caesar had written the entire account of the war at one time, it seems unlikely that each book would have been so self-contained. Furthermore, scholars have pointed to differences in style between the first and seventh books. This suggests a period of composition that stretched over years rather than weeks or months.

When the *Commentaries* on the Gallic War were published is equally disputed. On the one hand it has been argued that Caesar, in his desire to influence public opinion in Rome and to remind the reading public of his achievements, would have published each book as it was completed, or, to the same end, small groups of books. On the other the date of publication has been tied to Caesar's possible intention to stand for the consulship of 49 B.C. The elections for this were to take place in the summer of 50 B.C., and according to this interpretation the entire seven books, whether written at one time or in stages, would have been published with a view to influencing public opinion in 51 or early 50 B.C.

Caesar's Gallic Commands

Julius Caesar held his first consulship in 59 B.C. Shortly before this he had entered into a political alliance (*amicitia*) with Pompey the Great (Cn. Pompeius Magnus), Rome's greatest general at the time and Marcus Crassus, perhaps the richest Roman of the day. Historians have called this arrangement the First Triumvirate, but it should be noted that unlike the later Second Triumvirate of Mark Antony, Lepidus and Octavian, which was legally constituted, this was never more than an unofficial, private (and at first secret) coalition between three men "to work together for their mutual political advantage".[10]

Caesar as consul first fulfilled through his agent, the tribune Publius Vatinius, his obligations to his partners, who had helped secure his election. In Pompey's case his recently concluded settlement of the Near East was ratified; in Crassus's the financial obligation of a company of Asian tax-collectors, who had Crassus's support, was reduced by one-third. The Senate's reluctance to approve these measures had been instrumental in the formation of the political alliance. He then turned to his own affairs.

Prior to the consular elections for 59 B.C. the Senate, in order to block Caesar's future career, had assigned to him, as a proconsular province for the year 58 B.C., instead of an overseas command, the *silvae callesque* of Italy - supervision of the forests and cattle-pastures.[11] Vatinius changed this by carrying a bill through the popular assembly that gave Caesar the governorship of Cisalpine Gaul (*Gallia Cisalpina*) and Illyricum for five years along with three legions. Later in 59 B.C., when the governor-elect of Narbonese Gaul died unexpectedly, the Senate on Pompey's proposal granted him this province too with one more legion, since it realized that Caesar could secure it for himself in the popular assembly through the agency of Vatinius or another friendly tribune. His operations in Gaul began early in 58 B.C.

In 56 B.C. Caesar, Pompey and Crassus met at Luca in Cisalpine Gaul where, in spite of differences that had emerged in the preceding years, their *amicitia* was confirmed. The following year, as part of the agreement that emerged at Luca, Pompey and Crassus sponsored a law that extended Caesar's Gallic command for a further five years.

Caesar's time in Gaul - nine years in all - unquestionably formed the basis of his later ascendancy. He acquired, as "the greatest brigand of them all", huge amounts of war-booty that enabled him to buy political services in Rome on the scale of Crassus.[12] Furthermore, he emerged with a seasoned army of veterans that was devoted to its commander and willing to follow him across and beyond the Rubicon.

The Nomenclature of Gaul

Gallia Cisalpina

This was the fertile region of northern Italy between the Alps and the Appenines. Gallic tribes had migrated into this territory about 400 B.C. From here they raided Italy southwards, one attack resulting in the capture and sack of Rome (390 B.C.). Colonization by Rome and the Italianization of the area followed the eventual defeat of the Gauls, and

Gallia Cisalpina also became known as *Gallia Togata*. *Gallia Cisalpina* was established as a province in the eighties B.C. (the exact date is uncertain). The term *Gallia Cisalpina* was employed in official language, but in the everyday parlance of the first century B.C. the term *Italia* was understood to include the sub-Alpine lands of northern Italy.[13]

Gallia Transalpina

In its broadest application *Gallia Transalpina* referred to all of Gaul across the Alps, a territory comprising in modern terms France, Belgium, southern Holland, Germany west of the Rhine and most of Switzerland.

A belt of territory in the southeast was annexed as a province in 121 B.C. This province was called *Gallia Transalpina*, later *Gallia Narbonensis* (after the colony Narbo). It was also referred to simply as the *Provincia*, a practice that is reflected in the modern French name for the area, Provence.

Transalpine Gaul excluding the province was also called *Gallia Comata* ('longhaired Gaul') by the Romans.

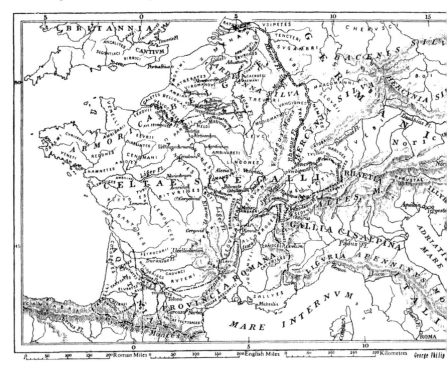

GAUL IN CAESAR'S TIME

Footnotes for Introduction

1. The most valuable discussion is in F.E. Adcock, *Caesar as a Man of Letters* (1956), pp.6ff.; R.M. Ogilvie's chapter on Caesar in the *Cambridge History of Classical Literature*, vol. II (1982), pp.281ff. is also useful.

2. See J.P.V.D. Balsdon, 'The Veracity of Caesar', *Greece and Rome* (1957), p.20; the *litterae* are mentioned at the end of books II, IV and VII.

3. A.N. Sherwin-White, 'Caesar as an Imperialist', *Greece and Rome* (1957), p.36

4. For Caesar are, e.g., A.N. Sherwin-White, *Journal of Roman Studies* (1958), pp.188ff., J.P.V.D. Balsdon, *Journal of Roman Studies* (1955), pp.161ff. and R.M. Ogilvie, op. cit., p.282; against Caesar are, e.g., G. Walser, *Caesar und die Germanen* (1956), and M. Rambaud, *L'Art de la Déformation Historique dans les Commentaires de Cesar* (1953).

5. *From the Gracchi to Nero* (1970), p.427

6. *voluit alios habere parata, unde sumerent qui vellent scribere historiam, Brutus* 75,262

7. *sanos quidem homines a scribendo deterruit; nihil est in historia pura et inlustri brevitate dulcius,* ibid.

8. F.E. Adcock, op. cit., p.13; so too R.M. Ogilvie, op. cit., p.284: "Caesar elevated the Commentary into a literary form in its own right. It was no longer merely raw material for history".

9. See Adcock, op. cit., pp.77ff.; Ogilvie, op. cit., pp.281-2.

10. H.H. Scullard, op. cit., p.118

11. Suetonius, *Julius Caesar*, 19

12. The quotation is from E. Badian, *Roman Imperialism in the Late Republic* (1968), p.89; see also M. Cary and H.H. Scullard, *A History of Rome* (1975), p.265.

13. M. Cary and H.H. Scullard, op. cit., p.140; see also *Oxford Classical Dictionary* (1978), s.v. 'Cisalpine Gaul'.

BOOK I

I.1,1-4 The three divisions of Gaul

Caesar in the opening sentences of his *Commentaries* rightly draws attention to the variety that existed among the Gallic peoples. Yet, in spite of their differences, these peoples had many cultural elements in common. The inhabitants of Gaul were part of a widespread 'Celtic' culture in Europe that stretched, at its fullest expansion in the second century B.C., from Ireland and parts of the Iberian peninsula in the west to Romania in the east; from northern Italy in the south to the Danube in the north. The Celts who entered Gaul and eventually outnumbered the original inhabitants began crossing the Rhine from about 800 B.C.

Caesar remarks that the people who called themselves *Celtae* were called *Galli* by the Romans. In fact the inhabitants of northwestern Europe were commonly referred to interchangeably as Celts or Gauls by both Greek and Roman writers.[1]

The word *Gallia* is used by Caesar in different senses in his *Commentaries*. On the one hand it may, as it does in the famous opening sentence of the first book, refer to all of *Gallia Comata*. On the other hand he uses it in a more restricted sense to refer to the part inhabited by the people who called themselves *Celtae*.[2]

> Gallia est omnis divisa in partes tres, quarum unam incolunt Belgae, aliam Aquitani, tertiam qui ipsorum lingua Celtae, nostra Galli appellantur. Hi omnes lingua, institutis, legibus inter se differunt. Gallos ab Aquitanis Garumna flumen, a Belgis Matrona et Sequana dividit. Horum omnium 5
fortissimi sunt Belgae, propterea quod a cultu atque humanitate provinciae longissime absunt, minimeque ad eos mercatores saepe commeant atque ea quae ad effeminandos animos pertinent important, proximique sunt Germanis qui trans Rhenum incolunt, quibuscum continenter bellum 10
gerunt. Qua de causa Helvetii quoque reliquos Gallos virtute praecedunt, quod fere cotidianis proeliis cum Germanis contendunt, cum aut suis finibus eos prohibent aut ipsi in eorum finibus bellum gerunt.

Note on the vocabulary lists:

An asterisk indicates the first occurrence of a word that will recur in these selections. These are words that should be known by the end of the first two years of Latin, and they will not be listed again. If they are forgotten, they can be looked up in Appendix B.

I.1,1-4

pars, partis (f) : part; side, direction
incolo, -colere, -colui : inhabit, live in; cultivate
Belgae, -arum (m pl) : the Belgae (inhabitants of the north of Gaul)
alius, -a, -ud : another, other
Aquitani, -orum (m pl) : the Aquitani (inhabitants of the southwestern part of Gaul)
tertius, -a, -um : third
lingua, -ae (f) : language; tongue (*ipsorum lingua* (1.2) - translate 'in their language'; *lingua* (1.3) is an ablative of respect, as are *institutis* and *legibus*; translate 'in language...')
Celtae, -arum (m pl) : the Celts
Galli, -orum (m pl) : the Gauls
appello (1) : call
institutum, -i (n) : custom
lex, legis (f) : law
inter : among, between (preposition with accusative)
differo, -ferre, distuli, dilatum : differ; spread, scatter; delay
Garumna, -ae (f) : the Garonne river
flumen, -inis (n) : river
Matrona, -ae (f) : the Marne river
Sequana, -ae (f) : the Seine river
propterea quod : because
cultus, -us (m) : civilization, culture
humanitas, -atis (f) : culture, refinement; humanity; human nature; kindness
provinciae : Caesar means the Roman province of Gallia Narbonensis
longissime : furthest (superlative adverb formed from *longus, -a, -um*)
absum, -esse, afui : be distant, be away
minime : take with *saepe*; translate 'hardly at all'
commeo (1) : visit, go to
effemino (1) : weaken, make effeminate
animus, -i (m) : spirit; mind; soul
pertineo, -tinere, -tinui : pertain, concern; extend
importo (1) : import, bring in
proximus, -a, -um : nearest, next; last
Germani, -orum (m pl) : the Germans (for the identity of the Germans see introduction to VI.21)
Rhenus, -i (m) : the Rhine river

continenter : continually
*bellum gero, gerere, gessi, gestum : wage war
qua de causa : for this reason
*Helvetii, -orum (m pl) : the Helvetii (inhabitants of what is now
    Switzerland; the Helvetic name is still reflected in the modern
    names for the Swiss Confederation: 'Confederation Helvetique' and
    'Confederatio Helvetica' in French and German respectively)
*reliquus, -a, -um : remaining, rest, left
*virtus, -utis (f) : bravery, courage; manliness; virtue
praecedo, -cedere, -cessi, -cessum : surpass; go before, precede
*fere : almost, nearly; usually, in general
*cotidianus, -a, -um : daily
*proelium, -i (n) : battle
*contendo, -tendere, -tendi, -tentum : fight, contend; hurry; strain
*finis, -is (m) : limit, boundary; in plural, as here, = 'territory'
*prohibeo, -hibere, -hibui, -hibitum : keep from, prevent, hinder

Caesar's first involvement in *Gallia Comata* - the expulsion of the Helvetii (57 B.C.)

The chapters that follow the description of the geography and inhabitants of Gaul deal with the migration of the Celtic tribe, the Helvetii, from their homeland in modern Switzerland into *Gallia Comata*. In these chapters Caesar carefully explains and justifies his involvement in Gaul outside of his province.[3] He does this to preempt charges that his enemies at Rome might bring against him under either of two laws: the *Lex Cornelia maiestatis* or the *Lex Iulia repetendarum*. Both these laws regulated the conduct of provincial governors, and the former specifically forbade a governor from taking an army outside of his province without permission from the Senate.

The essentials of Caesar's case are as follows:

- in opposing the Helvetii in their plan to move into Gaul and in pursuing them when they did so, he was acting on the principle of punishing old enemies of Rome, who in this case had in 107 B.C. killed a consul and forced his army to pass under the yoke (I.7);

- the Helvetii, in planning to settle in the territory of the Santones, posed a potential threat to the rich farmland around Tolosa (modern Toulouse) in the south of *Gallia Narbonensis* (I.10);

- in helping the Aedui, who were old allies of Rome, the Ambarri and the Allobroges against the Helvetii (I.11), he was following the long established practice of defending Rome's allies.[4]

I.2; I.3,1-2 The conspiracy of Orgetorix in 61 B.C. and his persuasion of the Helvetii to emigrate

Caesar's account of the migration of the Helvetii shows that the population movements that had brought Celtic peoples into Gaul still continued. "They were a population in a state of flux. Pressure on land was still intense and the migratory movements of the previous centuries were far from over....Caesar's detailed analysis of the preparations of the Helvetii offers a unique insight into the causes and mechanisms of Celtic migration."[5]

I.2

Apud Helvetios longe nobilissimus fuit et ditissimus Orgetorix. Is, M. Messala et M. Pupio Pisone consulibus, regni cupiditate inductus coniurationem nobilitatis fecit, et civitati persuasit ut de finibus suis cum omnibus copiis exirent: perfacile esse, cum virtute omnibus praestarent, 5
totius Galliae imperio potiri. Id hoc facilius eis persuasit, quod undique loci natura Helvetii continentur: una ex parte flumine Rheno latissimo atque altissimo, qui agrum Helvetium a Germanis dividit; altera ex parte monte Iura altissimo, qui est inter Sequanos et Helvetios; tertia lacu 10
Lemanno et flumine Rhodano, qui provinciam nostram ab Helvetiis dividit. His rebus fiebat ut et minus late vagarentur et minus facile finitimis bellum inferre possent: qua ex parte homines bellandi cupidi magno dolore adficiebantur. Pro multitudine autem hominum et pro gloria belli atque 15
fortitudinis angustos se fines habere arbitrabantur, qui in longitudinem milia passuum CCXL, in latitudinem CLXXX patebant.

I.2
apud : among (preposition with accusative)
longe : by far
ditissimus, -a, -um : richest (from *dives, divitis*)
Orgetorix, -igis (m) : Orgetorix (a Helvetian noble)
M. Messala et M. Pupio Pisone consulibus : ablative absolute; translate
        'during the consulship of...' (Messala and Piso were consuls in 61
        B.C.)
regnum, -i (n) : royal power; kingdom; supremacy
cupiditas, -atis (f) : desire
induco, -ducere, -duxi, -ductum : persuade, induce; lead in
coniuratio, -onis (f) : conspiracy

nobilitas, -atis (f) : nobility

**civitas, -atis (f)* : state; citizenship; translate *civitati* 'the community'

**persuadeo, -suadere, -suasi, -suasum* : persuade (with dative of
    person(s) persuaded)

**copia, -ae (f)* : supply, plenty; in plural, as here, = 'forces, troops'

5   *perfacilis, -e* : very easy (*perfacile esse* is accusative and infinitive
    construction depending on a verb of saying that is understood from
    persuasit)

**praesto, -stare, -stiti, -stitum* : be superior; show

**totus, -a, -um* : all, whole, entire (genitive = *totius*)

imperium, -i (n) : command, power; empire

potior, -iri, -itus sum : gain possession of, acquire (here with ablative)

id hoc facilius eis persuasit : very literally 'he persuaded this (*id -*
    accusative) to them (*eis*) more easily through this (*hoc -* ablative)';
    persuadeo often takes a neuter accusative pronoun in addition to a
    dative of person

*undique : on all sides, from all sides

contineo, -tinere, -tinui, -tentum : shut in; contain, hold

una ex parte : translate 'on one side' (*ex* is used similarly in 1.9 in the
    phrase *altera ex parte*)

**latus, -a, -um* : broad

**alter, -era, -erum* : the other; one (of two)

Iura, -ae (f) : the Jura mountain range

10 **Sequani, -orum (m pl)* : the Sequani (a Gallic tribe living west of the
    Jura)

lacus, -us (m) : lake

Lemannus, -i (m) : lake Geneva

**Rhodanus, -i (m)* : the Rhone river

**fio, fieri, factus sum* : come about, happen; become, be made

minus : less

vagor, -ari, -atus sum : wander, roam (*vagarentur* is subjunctive as the
    verb of a noun clause of result, introduced by *ut*, that is the subject
    of *fiebat*; *possent* is subjunctive for the same reason; noun clauses
    function in the same way as nouns do, i.e. as subjects or objects of
    verbs)

**finitimus, -a, -um* : neighboring, adjacent; the plural *finitimi, -orum (m)*
    is used, as here, as a noun = 'neighbors'

**bellum infero, -ferre, -tuli, inlatum* : make war on (with dative)

qua ex parte : translate 'for this reason'

**bello (1)* : wage war, fight

cupidus, -a, -um : desirous

dolor, -is (m) : sorrow, grief

**adficio, -ficere, -feci, -fectum* : affect; afflict

pro : translate both occurrences 'considering'

15 *multitudo, -inis (f) : great number, multitude
    gloria, -ae (f) : reputation; glory
    fortitudo, -inis (f) : bravery; strength (the genitive fortitudinis depends on
        gloria, as does belli; despite the genitives translate belli atque
        fortitudinis 'for war and bravery')
    angustus, -a, -um : narrow; close
    *arbitror, -ari, -atus sum : consider, think, judge
    *longitudo, -inis (f) : length
    *milia passuum : miles (literally 'thousands of paces')
    *latitudo, -inis (f) : width, breadth
    *pateo, -ere, -ui : extend; lie open, be exposed

I.3,1-2

His rebus adducti et auctoritate Orgetorigis permoti,
constituerunt ea quae ad proficiscendum pertinerent
comparare, iumentorum et carrorum quam maximum
numerum coemere, sementes quam maximas facere ut in
itinere copia frumenti suppeteret, cum proximis civitatibus   5
pacem et amicitiam confirmare. Ad eas res conficiendas
biennium sibi satis esse duxerunt: in tertium annum
profectionem lege confirmant.

I.3,1-2

adduco, -ducere, -duxi, -ductum : lead on, induce; lead to, bring to

auctoritas, -atis (f) : influence, authority

permoveo, -movere, -movi, -motum : influence, move deeply

constituo, -stituere, -stitui, -stitutum : decide, determine; establish

pertinerent : subjunctive in a relative clause of characteristic; they
    prepared things *of the sort* that related to their setting out

proficiscor, -ficisci, -fectus sum : set out, start

comparo (1) : prepare; put together

iumentum, -i (n) : draught-animal, beast of burden

carrus, -i (m) : baggage-wagon (with four wheels)

quam maximum numerum : translate 'the greatest possible number'

coemo, -emere, -emi, -emptum : buy up

sementes quam maximas facere : translate 'to sow as much corn as
    possible'

iter, itineris (n) : journey, march; route

frumentum, -i (n) : grain, wheat, corn

suppeto, -petere, -petii (or -ivi), -petitum : be sufficient; be at hand

pax, pacis (f) : peace

amicitia, -ae (f) : friendship

confirmo (1) : secure, strengthen; confirm; of public affairs 'resolve,
    ratify' (thus in 1.8)

conficio, -ficere, -feci, -fectum : complete, carry through; wear out,
    exhaust

biennium, -i (n) : a period of two years

duxerunt : they considered (in addition to the basic meaning 'lead' *duco*
    also means 'consider')

in tertium annum : translate 'for the third year'

profectio, -onis (f) : departure, setting forth

I.7 Caesar hurries to Geneva

Caesar further bolstered his case for opposing the Helvetii by reminding his readers in this passage of the humiliating defeat of Lucius Cassius Longinus and his army.

This defeat occurred in Southern Gaul in 107 B.C. The Helvetii had reinforced two Germanic tribes, the Cimbri and Teutones, when they migrated into Gaul in search of a new home. The Roman general Marius defeated the Teutones at Aquae Sextiae (Aix-en-Provence) in *Gallia Narbonensis* in 102 B.C. and the Cimbri in northern Italy in 101 B.C., but only after they had struck fear into Roman hearts by defeating five Roman armies and penetrating into *Gallia Narbonensis* and across the Alps into Italy.[6]

This is the first instance of what is a recurrent theme in the *Commentaries*: the danger represented to Gaul and Rome by German tribes. There can be little doubt that Caesar played up this threat as a way of justifying his military campaigns.[7]

Caesari cum id nuntiatum esset, eos per provinciam nostram iter facere conari, maturat ab urbe proficisci, et quam maximis potest itineribus in Galliam ulteriorem contendit, et ad Genavam pervenit. Provinciae toti quam maximum potest militum numerum imperat (erat omnino in Gallia ulteriore   5 legio una), pontem qui erat ad Genavam iubet rescindi. Ubi de eius adventu Helvetii certiores facti sunt, legatos ad eum mittunt nobilissimos civitatis, cuius legationis Nammeius et Verucloetius principem locum obtinebant, qui dicerent sibi esse in animo sine ullo maleficio iter per provinciam facere,   10 propterea quod aliud iter haberent nullum: rogare ut eius voluntate id sibi facere liceat. Caesar, quod memoria tenebat L. Cassium consulem occisum exercitumque eius ab Helvetiis pulsum et sub iugum missum, concedendum non putabat; neque homines inimico animo, data facultate per   15 provinciam itineris faciendi, temperaturos ab iniuria et maleficio existimabat. Tamen, ut spatium intercedere posset dum milites quos imperaverat convenirent, legatis respondit diem se ad deliberandum sumpturum: si quid vellent, ad Id. April. reverterentur.   20

I.7

nuntio (1) : report, announce

*conor, -ari, -atus sum : try

maturo (1) : hurry; ripen

quam maximis potest itineribus : translate 'with the longest marches
     possible'

*ulterior, -ius : further (by *Galliam ulteriorem* Caesar means *Gallia
     Narbonensis*)

Genava, -ae (f) : Geneva

*pervenio, -venire, -veni, -ventum : reach, arrive at

quam maximum potest militum numerum : translate 'the greatest number
     of soldiers possible'

*impero (1) : requisition, levy (with accusative of thing demanded, dative
     of source demanded from); order, command (with dative)(this
     latter is the more common meaning of the word)

*omnino : altogether

*legio, -onis (f) : legion (at full strength six thousand men)

*pons, pontis (m) : bridge

*iubeo, -ere, iussi, iussum : order

rescindo, -scindere, -scidi, -scissum : cut down

*adventus, -us (m) : arrival

*certiorem facio, -ere, feci, factum : inform (literally 'make x more
     certain'; here the passive is used)

*legatus, -i (m) : envoy, ambassador; deputy, second-in-command

legatio, -onis (f) : embassy, legation

princeps, -ipis : foremost, chief; as a noun 'leader; emperor'

obtineo, -tinere, -tinui, -tentum : hold, maintain; obtain

qui dicerent : translate 'who were to say' (a relative clause of purpose)

*esse in animo : to intend (often with dative of person(s) intending)

*ullus, -a, -um : any

*maleficium, -i (n) : wrongdoing, harm, mischief

haberent : subjunctive as the verb of a subordinate clause in indirect
     speech

*nullus, -a, -um : no, none

rogare : understand *se*; translate '(they said) that they were asking'
     (accusative and infinitive construction depending on an implied
     verb of saying)

*voluntas, -atis (f) : consent; wish, will

*licet, -ere, -uit (or *licitum est*) : it is permitted (impersonal verb)

*teneo, -ere, -ui, tentum : hold; maintain; *memoria* (ablative) *tenere* =
     'remember'

*occido, -cidere, -cidi, -cisum : kill (with *occisum, pulsum* and *missum*
     understand *esse*)

*exercitus, -us (m) : army

*pello, -ere, pepuli, pulsum : rout; strike; drive

iugum, -i (n) : yoke, collar (of oxen etc.); ridge; it may also refer, as it does here, to a crossbar or spear under which an army might be forced to pass as a mark of submission

concedo, -cedere, -cessi, -cessum : allow, concede; withdraw (*concedendum* is a gerundive of obligation - 'that it should be allowed')

15 *puto (1)* : think, consider, judge

inimicus, -a, -um : hostile; as noun *inimicus, -i (m)*, or
  inimica, -ae (f) = 'enemy'

facultas, -atis (f) : opportunity

tempero (1) : refrain, control oneself; restrain (with *temperaturos* understand *esse*)

iniuria, -ae (f) : wrong, injustice, injury

existimo (1) : think; estimate

spatium, -i (n) : interval, time; space, distance

intercedo, -cedere, -cessi, -cessum : intervene, come between

dum : until

convenio, -venire, -veni, -ventum : assemble, meet, come together; agree (the subjunctive *convenirent* with *dum* is used to denote something anticipated or expected)

delibero (1) : deliberate

sumo, -ere, sumpsi, sumptum : take (with *sumpturum* understand *esse*)

si...quid : if...anything

Id. April. : the Ides of April (the 13th)

20 *revertor, -verti, -versus sum* : return; translate *reverterentur* 'they should return' (*reverterentur* is subunctive in indirect speech for what would have been an imperative in Caesar's actual words)

A note on Caesar's army

The backbone of Caesar's army in Gaul was the force of legions under his command. The number of legions he had during the Gallic campaigns fluctuated between six and eleven. In addition to these he had cavalry (a force of five thousand is mentioned at one point in the *Commentaries* (IV.12,1)) and an unspecified number of auxiliary troops - slingers, archers, light-armed infantry - who like the cavalry were foreigners.

At full strength a legion consisted of six thousand men, all Roman citizens except in emergency situations when non-citizens were enrolled. However, frequently a legion's numbers were not up to nominal strength and this was the case with Caesar's legions in Gaul. Each legion at full strength had ten cohorts of six hundred men; each cohort three maniples of two hundred; and each maniple two centuries of a hundred men. At this time the legionaries were volunteers recruited by the generals who needed their service. Since they were paid by their commander and not from the state treasury, they tended to owe their loyalty to him and not to the state, which needless to say had grave political implications.

The commanding officer of a legion was the *legatus legionis*, who was a man of senatorial rank. Beneath the *legatus* there were six military tribunes for each legion. These were usually young men without military experience, for whom the position was a recognized step in a political career. This office was mainly administrative and in battle the tribunes were not nearly as important as the centurions, of whom there were sixty to a legion. There were grades of centurions and these men commanded not just centuries, as the name implies, but, commensurate with their rank, maniples or cohorts. The most senior centurions were present at councils of war and involved in general command.

I.9 Dumnorix secures passage for the Helvetii

With the help of Dumnorix, the Aeduan, the Helvetii secured permission from the Sequani to pass through their territory. This indicates that not all members of the Aeduan nobility were committed to their state's alliance with Rome. "The facts suggest that he [Dumnorix] was really the leader of a popular party which opposed, in the national interest, the pro-Roman policy of the Aeduan nobles."[8]

After Caesar's defeat of the Helvetii Dumnorix was spared by Caesar as a favor to his pro-Roman brother, Diviciacus.

> Relinquebatur una per Sequanos via, qua Sequanis invitis
> propter angustias ire non poterant. His cum sua sponte
> persuadere non possent, legatos ad Dumnorigem Aeduum
> mittunt, ut eo deprecatore a Sequanis impetrarent. Dumnorix
> gratia et largitione apud Sequanos plurimum poterat, et   5
> Helvetiis erat amicus, quod ex ea civitate Orgetorigis filiam
> in matrimonium duxerat et, cupiditate regni adductus, novis
> rebus studebat et quam plurimas civitates suo beneficio
> habere obstrictas volebat. Itaque rem suscipit et a Sequanis
> impetrat ut per fines suos Helvetios ire patiantur, obsidesque 10
> uti inter sese dent perficit: Sequani, ne itinere Helvetios
> prohibeant; Helvetii, ut sine maleficio et iniuria transeant.

I.9

relinquo, -linquere, -liqui, -lictum : leave, abandon

invitus, -a, -um : unwilling

propter : on account of (preposition with accusative)

angustiae, -arum (f pl) : narrowness; difficulty

sua sponte : by themselves, by their own efforts; voluntarily

Dumnorix, -igis (m) : Dumnorix (an Aeduan noble)

Aeduus, -a, -um: Aeduan; as a noun *Aeduus, -i (m)* = 'an Aeduan'; in
      plural 'the Aedui', a powerful Gallic tribe

deprecator, -oris (m) : intermediary (*eo deprecatore* is an ablative
      absolute)

impetro (1) : get one's way, obtain by asking; accomplish

gratia, -ae (f) : popularity, agreeableness; favor; thankfulness; grace;
      translate *gratia* 'because of his popularity' (it is an ablative of
      cause; so too *largitione*)

largitio, -onis (f) : generosity; bribery

plurimum poterat : translate 'had much influence'

in matrimonium duco, -ere, duxi, ductum : marry

res novae, rerum novarum (f pl) : revolution

studeo, -ere, -ui : be eager; study (with dative)

quam plurimas civitates : translate 'as many tribes as possible'

beneficium, -i (n) : kindness, favor

obstringo, -stringere, -strinxi, -strictum : bind, tie

suscipio, -cipere, -cepi, -ceptum : undertake

patior, pati, passus sum : allow; suffer (*ut...patiantur* is a noun clause of
      result, object of *impetrat*; hence the verb is subjunctive)

obses, -idis, (c) : hostage (*obsides* is the object of *dent*)

uti : for *ut* (*uti...dent* is a noun clause of result, object of *perficit*)

perficio, -ficere, -feci, -fectum : bring about, finish

transeo, -ire, -ii (or *-ivi*), *-itum* : cross, go over

I.10 Caesar enters *Gallia Comata*

Again Caesar justifies his involvement outside of his province: if the Helvetii settled in the territory of the Santones, part of the province would be threatened.

Caesar may in this passage have exaggerated the proximity of the Santones to the Tolosates. The distance from the closest frontier of the Santones to Tolosa (modern Toulouse), the chief town of the Tolosates, was 130 miles. It was, however, an open route with no obstacles to an army on the march.[9]

> Caesari renuntiatur Helvetiis esse in animo per agrum
> Sequanorum et Aeduorum iter in Santonum fines facere, qui
> non longe a Tolosatium finibus absunt, quae civitas est in
> provincia. Id si fieret, intellegebat magno cum periculo
> provinciae futurum ut homines bellicosos, populi Romani   5
> inimicos, locis patentibus maximeque frumentariis finitimos
> haberet. Ob eas causas ei munitioni quam fecerat T.
> Labienum legatum praefecit; ipse in Italiam magnis
> itineribus contendit, duasque ibi legiones conscribit, et tres
> quae circum Aquileiam hiemabant ex hibernis educit et, qua   10
> proximum iter in ulteriorem Galliam per Alpes erat, cum eis
> quinque legionibus ire contendit. Ibi Ceutrones et Graioceli
> et Caturiges, locis superioribus occupatis, itinere exercitum
> prohibere conantur. Compluribus eis proeliis pulsis ab
> Ocelo, quod est citerioris provinciae extremum, in fines   15
> Vocontiorum ulterioris provinciae die septimo pervenit; inde
> in Allobrogum fines, ab Allobrogibus in Segusiavos
> exercitum ducit. Hi sunt extra provinciam trans Rhodanum
> primi.

I.10

renuntio (1) : report

*Santones, -um (m pl) or Santoni, -orum : the Santones (a tribe of the
    coast of Gaul)

Tolosates, -ium (m pl) : the Tolosates (inhabitants of Tolosa, modern
    Toulouse, a town in *Gallia Narbonensis*)

fieret : subjunctive in a subordinate clause in indirect speech after
    intellegebat

*intellego, -legere, -lexi, -lectum : understand, perceive

*periculum, -i (n) : danger

5 *futurum* : understand *esse*, 'to be about to be' (the future infinitive of
    sum)

bellicosus, -a, -um : warlike, bellicose

maxime : very, most, especially; translate *maxime frumentariis* 'very rich in corn'

haberet : the subject of the verb is the province; *ut...haberet* is a noun clause, subject of *futurum (esse)*

ob : because of, on account of (preposition with accusative)

munitio, -onis (f) : fortification; building

T. Labienum : Titus Atius Labienus, Caesar's great second-in-command in Gaul (who later opposed him in the Civil War)

praeficio, -ficere, -feci, -fectum : put x (in accusative) in command of y (in dative)

magnis itineribus : translate 'by forced marches'

ibi : there

conscribo, -scribere, -scripsi, -scriptum : enlist; write

10 *circum* : around, about (preposition with accusative)

Aquileia, -ae (f) : Aquileia (a town in northeast Italy)

hiemo (1) : spend the winter

hiberna, -orum (n pl) : winter quarters

educo, -ducere, -duxi, -ductum : lead out; raise up; educate

qua : where

proximum : here translate 'shortest'

ulteriorem Galliam : again Caesar means *Gallia Narbonensis*

Alpes, -ium (f pl) : the Alps

Ceutrones, -um (m pl) : the Ceutrones (a Gallic tribe)

Graioceli, -orum (m pl) : the Graioceli (a Gallic tribe)

Caturiges, -um (m pl) : the Caturiges (a Gallic tribe)

superior, -ius : higher, superior; former

occupo (1) : seize, capture; occupy

complures, -ium : several (*compluribus* goes with *proeliis*)

eis...pulsis : ablative absolute

15 *Ocelum, -i (n)* : Ocelum (a town of Cisalpine Gaul)

citerior, -ius : on this side; *citerior provincia* means Cisalpine Gaul, i.e. Gaul on the Italian side of the Alps

extremus, -a, -um : last, farthest (Caesar means that Ocelum was the last or farthest town of Cisalpine Gaul)

Vocontii, -orum (m pl) : the Vocontii (a tribe of *Gallia Narbonensis*)

inde : from there, from that place

Allobroges, -um (m pl) : the Allobroges (a tribe of *Gallia Narbonensis*)

Segusiavi, -orum (m pl) : the Segusiavi (a Gallic tribe living just beyond the provincial frontier)

extra : outside; beyond (preposition with accusative)

I.11 The Aedui and other tribes ask Caesar to protect them from the Helvetii

As mentioned previously Caesar takes care to point out that he was defending Roman allies in opposing the Helvetii. The Aedui had in fact been *socii et amici* of Rome since 111 B.C. During the Republic it was through a system of alliances of this sort that Rome's hegemony and influence extended far outside of her formally annexed provinces.[10]

Helvetii iam per angustias et fines Sequanorum suas copias
traduxerant, et in Aeduorum fines pervenerant eorumque
agros populabantur. Aedui, cum se suaque ab eis defendere
non possent, legatos ad Caesarem mittunt rogatum auxilium:
ita se omni tempore de populo Romano meritos esse ut   5
paene in conspectu exercitus nostri agri vastari, liberi eorum
in servitutem abduci, oppida expugnari non debuerint.
Eodem tempore Ambarri*, necessarii et consanguinei
Aeduorum, Caesarem certiorem faciunt sese, depopulatis
agris, non facile ab oppidis vim hostium prohibere. Item   10
Allobroges, qui trans Rhodanum vicos possessionesque
habebant, fuga se ad Caesarem recipiunt, et demonstrant sibi
praeter agri solum nihil esse reliqui. Quibus rebus adductus
Caesar non exspectandum sibi statuit dum, omnibus fortunis
sociorum consumptis, in Santonos Helvetii pervenirent.   15

* The Oxford Text has *Aedui Ambarri* here.

I.11

traduco, -ducere, -duxi, -ductum : lead across

populor, -ari, -atus sum : lay waste, devastate

rogatum : supine of purpose following a verb of motion; translate 'to ask for'

*auxilium, -i (n) : help, aid

mereor, -eri, -itus sum : deserve, earn, merit (*se...meritos esse* is accusative and infinitive construction following a verb of saying that is understood)

*paene : almost

*conspectus, -us (m) : sight, view

vasto (1) : devastate, lay waste

*liberi, -orum (m pl) : children

*servitus, -utis (f) : slavery, servitude

abduco, -ducere, -duxi, -ductum : lead away, take away

*oppidum, -i (n) : town

*expugno (1) : capture; take by storm

debeo, -ere, -ui, -itum : owe; translate *non debuerint* 'ought not' (the subjects of the verb are *agri, liberi* and *oppida*)

Ambarri, -orum (m pl) : the Ambarri

necessarius, -i (m) : friend; kinsman

consanguinei, -orum (m pl) : relatives

depopulo (1) : lay waste, devastate

*vis, vis (f) : force, violence; plural *vires, virium* = 'strength'

*item : likewise; moreover

*vicus, -i (m) : village; a quarter or ward of a town

*fuga, -ae (f) : flight

*recipio, -cipere, -cepi, -ceptum : with a reflexive pronoun, as here, 'retreat'; alone = 'take back; receive'

demonstro (1) : point out, demonstrate

*praeter : except; besides; beyond (preposition with accusative)

*solum, -i (n) : soil; ground, bottom, floor

nihil...reliqui : translate 'nothing left' (*reliqui* is a partitive genitive following *nihil*)

exspecto (1) : wait for, expect

sibi (1.14) : dative of the agent with gerundive of obligation *exspectandum*

*statuo, -ere, -ui : decide; fix, set

dum : again = 'until' (for the subjunctive verb see under *convenirent* in I.7)

fortuna, -ae (f) : chance, luck, fortune; in plural, as here, = 'property, possessions'

socius, -i (m) : ally

consumo, -sumere, -sumpsi, -sumptum : destroy; use up, consume

I.28,3-5 The resettlement of the defeated Helvetii

The Helvetic migration came to an end with their defeat by Caesar and their forced repatriation.

When they had left their homeland in the first place, they had burnt their towns and villages and whatever food they were not taking with them. They had done so because they felt that they would face danger and hardship more bravely if there were no possibility of return.[11] It is because of this earlier destruction of property that we read in this passage of a devastated land in need of rebuilding. We note again the mention by Caesar of the danger represented to Roman interests by the Germans.

> Helvetios, Tulingos, Latovicos in fines suos, unde erant
> profecti, reverti iussit, et, quod omnibus frugibus amissis
> domi nihil erat quo famem tolerarent, Allobrogibus
> imperavit ut his frumenti copiam facerent: ipsos oppida
> vicosque, quos incenderant, restituere iussit. Id ea maxime   5
> ratione fecit, quod noluit eum locum unde Helvetii
> discesserant vacare, ne propter bonitatem agrorum Germani
> qui trans Rhenum incolunt e suis finibus in Helvetiorum
> fines   transirent   et   finitimi   Galliae   provinciae
> Allobrogibusque essent. Boios, petentibus Aeduis, quod   10
> egregia virtute erant cogniti, ut in finibus suis collocarent,
> concessit, quibus illi agros dederunt, quosque postea in
> parem iuris libertatisque condicionem atque ipsi erant
> receperunt.

I.28,3-5

Tulingi, -orum (m pl) : the Tulingi (neighbors of the Helvetii who had migrated with them)

Latovici, -orum (m pl) : the Latovici (neighbors of the Helvetii who also migrated with them)

*unde : from where, whence

fruges, -um (f pl) : crops, produce of the fields

*amitto, -mittere, -misi, -missum : lose; let go

fames, -is (f) : hunger; poverty

tolero (1) : endure, bear (*tolerarent* is subjunctive being the verb of a relative clause of characteristic; there was nothing of the *kind* or *sort* that would enable them to endure hunger)

facerent : translate 'provide'

5   *incendo, -cendere, -cendi, -censum* : set on fire, burn

restituo, -stituere, -stitui, -stitutum : restore, give back

*ratio, -onis (f) : reason; method, theory, plan; account; translate *ea maxime ratione* 'especially for this reason'

discedo, -cedere, -cessi, -cessum : depart, leave; separate
vaco (1) : be empty; be at leisure
bonitas, -atis (f) : excellence, good quality, goodness
10 *Boii, -orum (m pl)* : the Boii (they too had migrated with the Helvetii);
         Boios is object of *collocarent*
*peto, -ere, -ivi, -itum : request, entreat; seek; go after, make for
         (*petentibus Aeduis* - either ablative absolute or dative with
         concessit)
egregius, -a, -um : outstanding, distinguished; translate *egregia virtute*
         'for their outstanding courage'
*cognosco, -gnoscere, -gnovi, -gnitum : learn, get to know; translate
         erant cogniti 'they were known'
*colloco (1) : settle; position, arrange (the 'they' of the verb is the Aedui;
         ut...collocarent is the object of *concessit*)
quibus : the antecedent of the relative is *Boios*, which is also the
         antecedent of *quos*
*par, -is : equal, like
*ius, iuris (n) : right, justice, law
*libertas, -atis (f) : freedom, liberty
condicio, -onis (f) : condition; settlement, arrangement; place, rank
atque : here 'as' (with *parem*)

Footnotes for Book I :

1. A. & P. Wiseman, *The Battle for Gaul* (1980), p.10; S.A. Handford & J.F. Gardner, *Caesar - The Conquest of Gaul* (1982), p.12

2. Thus for example in I.2,2; see C.E. Stevens, 'The *Bellum Gallicum* as a Work of Propaganda', *Latomus* XI (1952), p.7 for further examples.

3. See especially M. Gelzer, *Caesar: Politician and Statesman* (1968), pp.104-5.

4. In *B.G.*, I.35 Caesar tells us, in connection with relations between the Aedui and the German leader Ariovistus, that the senate had in 61 B.C. passed a decree instructing the governor of Gaul to protect the Aedui and other friends of the Roman people.

5. A. & P. Wiseman, op. cit., p.11

6. For the Cimbric and Teutonic migrations see *Cambridge Ancient History*, vol. IX (1932), pp.139ff.

7. For further discussion of this see the opening remarks to IV.1.

8. S.A. Handford & J.F. Gardner, op. cit., p.228

9. T. Rice Holmes, *Caesar's Conquest of Gaul* (1911), p.225

10. The classic statement of this is E. Badian's magisterial *Foreign Clientelae 264-70 B.C.* (1958).

11. This is mentioned by Caesar in *B.G.*, I.5.

BOOK II

II.25 Caesar enters the battle against the Nervii

In 57 B.C., the second year of campaigning, Caesar fought the Belgic tribes of northwestern Gaul after they had taken up arms against him. In the opening of the first book he described these Belgic tribes as the fiercest in all Gaul, and the battle he fought against the Nervii was one of the most desperate he ever faced: "That day he overcame the Nervii".[1] He showed not only his great personal courage, but also his considerable inspirational qualities by, at a critical moment, entering the fray himself.

Caesar's conduct in this passage was not untypical of the man. "On the march he shared the hardships of the common soldier, striding on in front and not caring whether he exposed his bare head to rain or sun."[2]

This passage contains one of the longest sentences to be found in Caesar's writings. The Latin is not particularly difficult, but the sentence will need to be broken up into smaller parts in English.

Caesar ab decimae legionis cohortatione ad dextrum cornu profectus, ubi suos urgeri signisque in unum locum collatis duodecimae legionis confertos milites sibi ipsos ad pugnam esse impedimento vidit, quartae cohortis omnibus centurionibus occisis signiferoque interfecto, signo amisso,   5
reliquarum cohortium omnibus fere centurionibus aut vulneratis aut occisis, in his primipilo P. Sextio Baculo, fortissimo viro, multis gravibusque vulneribus confecto, ut iam se sustinere non posset, reliquos esse tardiores, et non nullos ab novissimis deserto proelio excedere ac tela vitare,   10
hostes neque a fronte ex inferiore loco subeuntes intermittere et ab utroque latere instare, et rem esse in angusto vidit, neque ullum esse subsidium quod summitti posset, scuto ab novissimis uni militi detracto, quod ipse eo sine scuto venerat, in primam aciem processit centurionibusque   15
nominatim appellatis, reliquos cohortatus milites, signa inferre et manipulos laxare iussit, quo facilius gladiis uti possent. Cuius adventu spe inlata militibus ac redintegrato animo, cum pro se quisque in conspectu imperatoris etiam in extremis suis rebus operam navare cuperet, paulum hostium   20
impetus tardatus est.

II.25

Translation pointers:

Take *ubi* (1.2) with *vidit* (1.4); before *reliquos esse tardiores* (1.9) understand *ubi vidit*; before *rem esse in angusto vidit* (1.12) understand *ubi*; *urgeri* (1.2) and all the infinitives in the first thirteen lines (with the exception of *sustinere* (1.9) and *summitti* (1.13)) are dependent on *vidit*, as the infinitives of accusative and infinitive constructions.

ab : here means 'after'
cohortatio, -onis (f) : encouragement, exhortation
dexter, -tra, -trum : right; skilful
*cornu, -us (n) : wing (of an army); horn
urgeo, -ere, ursi : press hard, push, urge
signum, -i (n) : standard; sign, signal
confero, -ferre, -tuli, collatum : bring together, put together; collect
confertus, -a, -um : crowded, packed
*pugna, -ae (f) : battle, fight
impedimentum, -i (n) : hindrance, impediment; *sibi...impedimento*, very
        literally 'were themselves (*ipsos*) for a hindrance (*impedimento*) to
        themselves (*sibi*) for battle' (*impedimento* is a predicative dative
        following a form of *sum*)
cohors, -tis (f) : cohort (there were ten cohorts, each of six hundred men,
        to a legion)
centurio, -onis (m) : centurion (a commander of a century, a company of
        one hundred men)
signifer, -i (m) : standard-bearer
interficio, -ficere, -feci, -fectum : kill
vulnero (1) : wound
primipilus, -i (m) : chief centurion
vulnus, -eris (n) : wound
confecto : translate 'exhausted'
*sustineo, -tinere, -tinui, -tentum : support, hold up; withstand, check
tardus, -a, -um : slow, tardy
*non nullus, -a, -um : some, several (often written as one word)
novissimi, -orum (m) : the rearguard, those at the rear; translate *ab
        novissimis* 'in the rear'
desero, -serere, -serui, -sertum : desert, abandon
*excedo, -cedere, -cessi, -cessum : go away, depart; exceed
*telum, -i (n) : weapon, dart, javelin
vito (1) : avoid
*frons, frontis (f) : front; forehead; translate *a fronte* 'in front'
*inferior, -ius : lower, inferior
subeo, -ire, -ii (or *-ivi*) : come up, approach; go under; undergo

intermitto, -mittere, -misi, -missum : pause, interrupt; leave free
uterque, -traque, -trumque : each, both
latus, -eris (n) : side
insto, -stare, -stiti : press closely; be close by
rem : translate 'the situation'
angustum, -i (n) : crisis; narrow space
subsidium, -i (n) : reinforcement, help, support
summitto, -mittere, -misi, -missum : send up; send as help; send under
posset : subjunctive in a relative clause of characteristic; there was no
     reinforcement of the *kind* that could be sent to help
scutum, -i (n) : shield
uni militi : the dative here conveys separation - 'from'
detraho, -trahere, -traxi, -tractum : pull away, take from; draw down
eo : there, to that place
15   *acies, aciei (f)* : line of battle; edge
procedo, -cedere, -cessi, -cessum : proceed, go forward
nominatim : by name
cohortor, -hortari, -hortatus sum : urge on, encourage
signa infero, -ferre, -tuli, inlatum : push forward
manipulus, -i (m) : maniple, company (there were three to a cohort)
laxo (1) : widen, open
quo : in order that (used in place of *ut* when a purpose clause contains a
     comparative)
gladius, -i (m) : sword
utor, uti, usus sum : use (with ablative)
spes, spei (f) : hope
infero : instil; bring in (for principal parts see *signa infero* above)
redintegro (1) : restore, renew
pro se : translate 'on behalf of himself'
quisque, quaeque, quidque : each, each one
imperator, -oris (m) : general, commander; emperor
etiam : even; also
in extremis suis rebus : translate 'in the gravest personal danger'
20   *operam navo (1)* : exert oneself, strive
cupio, -ire, -ii (or -ivi), -itum : desire, wish
paulum (also paulo) : a little, to some extent
impetus, -us (m) : attack; force
tardo (1) : slow down, delay

Footnotes for Book II :

1. Shakespeare, *Julius Caesar*, III,ii,177

2. M. Gelzer, op. cit., p.133 (following Suetonius, *Julius Caesar*, 57)

BOOK III

III.14,5-9; III.15,1-2 The naval battle against the Veneti

Military successes of 56 B.C. included the defeat of the powerful maritime tribe the Veneti. The Greek historian and geographer, Strabo, says that the Veneti opposed Caesar to prevent a Roman invasion of Britain that would interfere with their trade.[1] This trade with Britain is mentioned by Caesar himself.[2] If Strabo is correct, it appears that Caesar was by now planning his first expedition to Britain and that the Veneti had wind of it.

The tactics described by Caesar to board the enemy ships and turn a sea fight into a land fight bring to mind the *corvus* ('raven') that was successfully used by the Romans during the First Carthaginian War. "It was nothing more than a gangplank, thirty-six feet long and four feet wide, with a heavy spike at the outboard end....A vessel so equipped would warily keep its prow headed toward the enemy and, as soon as it closed in to ram, drop the 'raven'; the spike would embed in the deck, and a boarding force would rush over the plank."[3]

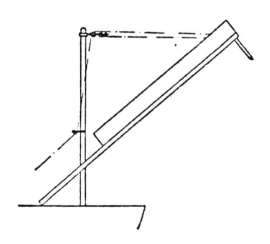

RECONSTRUCTION OF *CORVUS*

III.14,5-9

Una erat magno usui res praeparata a nostris, falces
praeacutae insertae adfixaeque longuriis, non absimili forma
muralium falcium. His cum funes qui antemnas ad malos
destinabant comprehensi adductique erant, navigio remis
incitato   praerumpebantur.   Quibus   abscisis   antemnae   5
necessario concidebant, ut, cum omnis Gallicis navibus spes
in velis armamentisque consisteret, his ereptis, omnis usus
navium uno tempore eriperetur. Reliquum erat certamen
positum in virtute, qua nostri milites facile superabant, atque
eo magis quod in conspectu Caesaris atque omnis exercitus   10
res gerebatur, ut nullum paulo fortius factum latere posset:
omnes enim colles ac loca superiora unde erat propinquus
despectus in mare ab exercitu tenebantur.

III.15,1-2

Disiectis ut diximus antemnis, cum singulas binae ac ternae
naves circumsteterant, milites summa vi transcendere in
hostium naves contendebant. Quod postquam barbari fieri
animadverterunt, expugnatis compluribus navibus, cum ei
rei nullum reperiretur auxilium, fuga salutem petere   5
contenderunt.

III.14,5-9

usus, -us (m) : use, advantage; practice; need; translate *magno usui* 'of
    great advantage' (*usui* is the predicative dative following a form of
    sum)
praeparo (1) : prepare
falx, -cis (f) : hook; sickle
praeacutus, -a, -um : sharpened, pointed
insero, -serere, -serui, -sertum : insert, introduce
adfigo, -figere, -fixi, -fixum : fasten, affix
longurius, -i (m) : long pole, rod
absimilis, -e : unlike
muralium falcium : translate 'siegehooks' (hooks or grappling irons used
    to pull down a wall during a siege)
his : ablative of means (the hooks attached to poles are meant)
funis, -is (m) : rigging, rope
antemna, -ae (f) : yardarm (the rod fastened across the mast to support
    the sail)
malus, -i (m) : mast

destino (1) : bind, tie down; designate

**comprehendo, -prehendere, -prehendi, -prehensum* : grasp, seize, arrest; comprehend

adducti erant : translate 'had been pulled tight'

navigium, -i (n) : ship

remus, -i (m) : oar

5   **incito (1)* : put in motion; rouse, urge on

praerumpo, -rumpere, -rupi, -ruptum : snap, break off

abscido, -scidere, -scidi, -scisum : cut off

**necessario* : necessarily

concido, -cidere, -cidi : fall down; perish

velum, -i (n) : sail; curtain

armamenta, -orum (n pl) : rigging

**consisto, -sistere, -stiti, -stitum* : depend on; consist of (both with *in* + ablative); halt, take a position

eripio, -ripere, -ripui, -reptum : snatch away, remove

certamen, -inis (n) : battle, contest

pono, -ere, posui, positum : place, put; translate *erat...positum in virtute* 'depended upon courage'

supero (1) : be superior; defeat

10 *eo magis* : so much the more

res : translate 'the engagement'

gero, -ere, gessi, gestum : carry out, conduct; display, wear

paulo fortius : translate 'a little braver (than usual)' *(fortius*, the neuter nominative singular of the comparative adjective, modifies *factum)*

factum, -i (n) : deed, act, exploit

lateo, -ere, -ui : escape notice, lie hidden

collis, -is (m) : hill

propinquuus, -a, -um : near, neighboring

despectus, -us (m) : view down

mare, -is (n) : sea

III.15,1-2

disicio, -icere, -ieci, -iectum : break up; scatter

**singuli, -ae, -a* : individual, single, one at a time

**bini, -ae, -a* : two at a time; two each

terni, -ae, -a : three at a time; three each

circumsisto, -sistere, -steti : surround, stand around

transcendo, -scendere, -scendi, -scensum : climb across; pass over

quod...fieri : accusative and infinitive construction following *animadverterunt* (*quod*, which is the neuter accusative singular of the relative pronoun, refers to the boarding of the ships as described in the previous sentence)

postquam : after

**animadverto, -vertere, -verti, -versum* : notice, pay attention to

5   *reperio, reperire, repperi, repertum* : find, find out, discover
    salus, -utis (f) : safety; health, well-being; salutation

Footnotes for Book III :

1. Strabo, IV.4,1

2. *B.G.,* III.8,1

3. L. Casson, *The Ancient Mariners* (1959), p.161; see also Polybius, I.22.

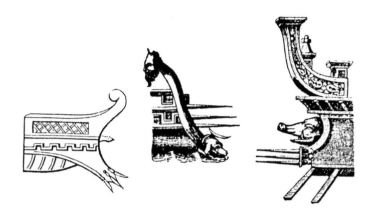

BOWS OF ANCIENT WAR GALLEYS WERE EQUIPPED WITH RAMS,
DEVICES USED TO SLAM INTO THE HULL OF AN ENEMY SHIP

ROMAN WARRIORS, ON THE DECK OF AN OARED WARSHIP EQUIPPED
WITH A TOWER, STAND READY TO FIGHT

BOOK IV

IV.1,3-10 The description of the Suebi

During his first year in Gaul after the Helvetic campaign Caesar drove Ariovistus, king of the German tribe the Suebi, back across the Rhine from land he and his followers were occupying. In 55 B.C. two other German tribes, the Usipetes and the Tencteri, crossed the Rhine under pressure from the Suebi. Before describing the hostilities with the Usipetes and the Tencteri and their defeat, Caesar writes about the character and customs of the Suebi. Those historians who believe that Caesar exaggerated the Germanic threat from across the Rhine and that he painted a picture of German barbarism to justify his aggressive military actions naturally see this passage as fitting that purpose.[1]

> Sueborum gens est longe maxima et bellicosissima
> Germanorum omnium. Hi centum pagos habere dicuntur, ex
> quibus quot annis singula milia armatorum bellandi causa ex
> finibus educunt. Reliqui qui domi manserunt se atque illos
> alunt; hi rursus in vicem anno post in armis sunt, illi domi   5
> remanent. Sic neque agri cultura nec ratio atque usus belli
> intermittitur. Sed privati ac separati agri apud eos nihil est,
> neque longius anno remanere uno in loco incolendi causa
> licet. Neque multum frumento sed maximam partem lacte
> atque pecore vivunt, multumque sunt in venationibus; quae   10
> res et cibi genere et cotidiana exercitatione et libertate vitae,
> quod a pueris nullo officio aut disciplina assuefacti nihil
> omnino contra voluntatem faciant, et vires alit et immani
> corporum magnitudine homines efficit. Atque in eam se
> consuetudinem adduxerunt ut locis frigidissimis neque   15
> vestitus praeter pelles haberent quicquam, quarum propter
> exiguitatem magna est corporis pars aperta, et lavantur in
> fluminibus.

IV.1,3-10

Suebi, -orum (m pl) : the Suebi (a Germanic tribe)
gens, gentis (f) : tribe; people; nation; clan
pagus, -i (m) : canton, district; village

quot annis : every year (also written as one word)
singula milia : i.e. a thousand armed men are taken from each canton
armati, -orum (m pl) : armed men
causa : for the sake of (with preceding genitive)
ex finibus : i.e. outside of their own territory
maneo, -ere, mansi, mansum : remain, stay
illos : i.e. the ones who are fighting
5 *alo, -ere, -ui, altum* : support; raise, nourish
hi : i.e. the ones who originally remained at home
rursus : again
in vicem : in turn (also written as one word)
remaneo : see *maneo* above
sic : in this way, thus
agri cultura, -ae (f) : agriculture (also written as one word)
ratio atque usus belli : translate 'military instruction and practice'
privati ac separati agri : partitive genitive dependent on *nihil*
agri : translate 'land'
maximam partem : translate 'for the greatest part' (it is an example of an
      adverbial accusative)
lac, lactis (n) : milk
10 *pecus, -oris (n)* : cattle
vivo, -ere, vixi, victum : live
venatio, -onis (f) : hunting, hunt
quae res : translate 'this practice' (it is the subject of *alit* and *efficit*)
cibus, -i (m) : food
genus, -eris (n) : kind, class; race; birth (*genere* is an ablative of cause,
      as are *exercitatione* and *libertate*)
exercitatio, -onis (f) : exercise, training
libertate vitae : translate 'freedom of lifestyle'
a pueris : translate 'from boyhood'
officium, -i (n) : duty, obligation; service; office
disciplina, -ae (f) : discipline; instruction; learning
assuefacio, -facere, -feci, -factum : train, accustom (used here with an
      ablative of means, *nullo officio aut disciplina*); *nullo...assuefacti*
      literally = 'trained by means of no duty or discipline'
contra : against; facing (preposition with accusative)
faciant : there is no strong reason for a subjunctive here and many
      editors emend the text to *faciunt*; possibly the sentence receives an
      indirect turn from the presence of *dicuntur* in l.2
immanis, -e : huge, enormous
corpus, -oris (n) : body
magnitudo, -inis (f) : size; greatness (*immani...magnitudine* is an
      ablative of description)
efficio, -ficere, -feci, -fectum : produce, bring about; achieve

15 *consuetudo, -inis (f)* : custom, habit

frigidus, -a, -um : cold; translate *locis frigidissimis* 'even in the coldest parts'

vestitus, -us (m) : clothing (*vestitus* is a partitive genitive dependent on *quicquam*)

*pellis, -is (f) : skin, hide

haberent : translate as present 'have' (imperfect by sequence of tenses following *adduxerunt*)

*quisquam, quaequam, quidquam (or *quicquam*) : anyone, anything

exiguitas, -atis (f) : scantiness, smallness

aperio, -ire, -ui, apertum : uncover, open

lavo, -are, lavi, lautum or lotum : wash; translate *lavantur* as 'bathe' (the passive functions as a middle)

IV.17,3-10 The bridge across the Rhine

In what was undoubtedly a show of Roman strength and capability Caesar determined to follow the defeat of the Germans with a crossing of the Rhine - by bridge rather than by boat since the latter would be beneath his dignity, the dignity that he later was to describe as dearer to him than life.[2] The bridge that was built in ten days, probably near modern Coblenz, is testimony to the skill of the engineers who accompanied the army. The account of its construction shows that Caesar was much more than a casual observer. "His evident fascination with the scheme, witnessed by the detail in which he describes it, suggests that he took a personal interest in the proceedings."[3]

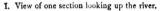
I. View of one section looking up the river.

II. View looking across the river.

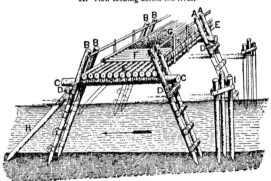

A, tigna bina sesquipedalia. *B*, his contraria duo. *C*, bipedales trabes. *D*, binae utrimque fibulae. *E*, directa materia. *F*, longurii. *G*, crates. *H*, sublicae obliquae. *I*, defensores.

PLAN OF CAESAR'S BRIDGE

IV.17,3-10

Rationem pontis hanc instituit. Tigna bina sesquipedalia
paulum ab imo praeacuta, dimensa ad altitudinem fluminis,
intervallo pedum duorum inter se iungebat. Haec cum
machinationibus immissa in flumen defixerat fistucisque
adegerat, non sublicae modo derecte ad perpendiculum sed   5
prone ac fastigate, ut secundum naturam fluminis
procumberent, eis item contraria duo ad eundem modum
iuncta intervallo pedum quadragenum ab inferiore parte
contra vim atque impetum fluminis conversa statuebat. Haec
utraque insuper bipedalibus trabibus immissis, quantum   10
eorum tignorum iunctura distabat, binis utrimque fibulis ab
extrema parte distinebantur; quibus disclusis atque in
contrariam partem revinctis, tanta erat operis firmitudo
atque ea rerum natura ut, quo maior vis aquae se
incitavisset, hoc artius inligata tenerentur. Haec derecta   15
materia iniecta contexebantur ac longuriis cratibusque
consternebantur; ac nihilo setius sublicae et ad inferiorem
partem fluminis oblique agebantur, quae pro ariete subiectae
et cum omni opere coniunctae vim fluminis exciperent, et
aliae item supra pontem mediocri spatio ut, si arborum   20
trunci sive naves deiciendi operis essent a barbaris missae,
his defensoribus earum rerum vis minueretur neu ponti
nocerent.

IV.17,3-10

rationem pontis hanc : translate 'this method of building the bridge'
*instituo, -stituere, -stitui, -stitutum : adopt; set in place; institute, begin,
    establish
tignum, -i (n) : timber, log, pile
sesquipedalis, -e : a foot and a half thick
imus, -a, -um : lowest; translate *ab imo* 'at the bottom ends'
praeacutus : sharpened, pointed
dimetior, -metiri, -mensus sum : measure off (the participle here has
    passive force)
*altitudo, -inis (f) : depth; height
intervallum, -i (n) : space, distance; interval
*pes, pedis (m) : foot
iungo, -ere, iunxi, iunctum : join
machinatio, -onis (f) : machine, machinery; cunning device
immitto, -mittere, -misi, -missum : let into, send into; send against

defigo, -figere, -fixi, -fixum : fix, plant securely

fistuca, -ae (f) : pile driver; hammer

adigo, -ere, -egi, -actum : drive home, thrust

sublica, -ae (f) : pile, stake

modus, -i (m) : manner, way; measure; *modo* with genitive = 'in the manner of'; thus *sublicae modo* = 'in the manner of a pile, like a pile'

derecte : straight (adverb from *derectus, -a, -um*, which is used in 1.15 with *materia* (1.16))

ad perpendiculum : translate 'vertically' (piles were usually driven in in this way)

prone : leaning, at an angle (adverb from *pronus, -a, -um*)

fastigate : sloping (adverb from *fastigatus, -a, -um*)

secundum : in the direction of; according to; after (preposition with accusative)

procumbo, -cumbere, -cubui, -cubitum : lean forward; sink down

eis...statuebat : the gist is that a second pair of logs was driven in forty feet downstream from and opposite to the first pair, inclining towards the current

contrarius, -a, -um : opposite, facing; contrary (with *contraria...duo* understand *tigna* - the case is accusative, object of *statuebat*)

quadrageni, -ae, -a : forty each (a genitive in *-enum*, as here, is used by Caesar)

ab inferiore parte : translate 'downstream'

converto, -vertere, -verti, -versum : turn; direct

haec utraque : translate 'these two pairs' (subject of *distinebantur*)

insuper : on top, above; in addition

bipedalis, -e : two feet thick

trabs, trabis (f) : beam, plank

quantum...distabat : literally 'as much as the joining of the timbers stood apart' (between each pair of timbers a beam two feet wide was placed that measured the distance between them)

utrimque : on each side, on both sides

fibula, -ae (f) : brace, bracket; brooch

ab extrema parte : translate 'on the outer side'

distineo, -tinere, -tinui, -tentum : keep apart

quibus : the antecedent must be *haec utraque* i.e. the pairs of timbers

discludo, -cludere, -clusi, -clusum : keep apart, shut off

in contrariam partem : translate 'in the opposite direction'

revincio, -vincire, -vinxi, -vinctum : bind fast; tie back

*tantus, -a, -um : so great, so much

*opus, -eris (n) : work

firmitudo, -inis (f) : strength, durability

ea rerum natura : translate 'the nature of the structure'

quo...hoc : Latin uses *quo...hoc...* or *quo...eo...* with a comparative in
   each clause to express English 'the more... the more...'

15 *artius* : more closely (comparative adverb from *artus, -a, -um*)

inligo (1) : bind, attach

haec : Caesar means the series of embedded timbers and crossbeams that
   straddled the river

*materia, -ae (f) : timber; material (*materia* is ablative of means; it is
   modified by *derecta* and *iniecta*)

inicio, -ere, -ieci, -iectum : place on; throw upon

contexo, -texere, -texui, -textum : connect together; weave together;
   translate *haec...contexebantur* 'these were connected together by
   straight boards laid over (them)' (Caesar is now referring to the
   connection in the direction of the bridge of the piles that had been
   set opposite each other)

longurius, -i (m) : long pole, rod

crates, -is (f) : wickerwork

consterno, -sternere, -stravi, -stratum : cover, spread over

nihilo setius : none the less (Caesar means that in spite of the work
   already described further construction was deemed necessary)

ad inferiorem partem fluminis : i.e. downstream from the bridge

oblique : obliquely, at an angle (adverb from *obliquus, -a, -um*)

ago, -ere, egi, actum : drive; do, act

pro ariete : translate 'as a buttress'

subicio, -ere, -ieci, -iectum : set below; throw under; throw up

coniungo, -iungere, -iunxi, -iunctum : join together

excipio, -cipere, -cepi, -ceptum : withstand, receive; take out, remove
   (*quae...exciperent* is a relative clause of purpose)

20 *supra* : above, over (preposition with accusative); translate *supra pontem*
   'upstream of the bridge'

mediocris, -e : moderate

truncus, -i (m) : trunk

sive : or; or if

deicio, -icere, -ieci, -iectum : demolish, throw down; translate *deiciendi
   operis* 'for the purpose of breaking down the structure'

defensor, -oris (m) : defender; translate *his defensoribus* 'with these (i.e.
   aliae sublicae) as barriers'

minuo, -ere, -ui, -utum : diminish, lessen

neu : and not; or not

noceo, -ere, -ui, nocitum : harm (with dative)

Caesar in Britain

potest videri ostendisse posteris, non tradidisse
(Tacitus, *Agricola* 13)

"it may be supposed that [Caesar] revealed [Britain] to his descendants,
rather than handed it over"

IV.20 Caesar's reasons for going to Britain

After the bridging of the Rhine, in autumn of the same year (55 B.C.)
Caesar undertook with two legions an exploratory trip to Britain.

He tells us that the Britons had been giving military aid to the Gauls. This
is correct but there was more to his trip than reconnaissance and a
demonstration of strength to the Britons. Britain was reputed to be a
country of great wealth, and if news of the expedition were favorably
received in Rome it was likely that a full-scale invasion would follow at a
later date.[4] There was also prestige that would accrue from such a
mission. "Probably an important motive was to secure the glory of leading
an army to victory on a distant and unknown island."[5]

Caesar's stay on the island was brief - a matter of weeks - and the
wrecking of his fleet by a storm placed the Romans in considerable
danger until the ships were rebuilt. However, the reaction in Rome was
indeed favorable. Upon receipt of the report of the year's campaigning the
Senate decreed a public thanksgiving of twenty days.

> Exigua parte aestatis reliqua Caesar, etsi in his locis, quod
> omnis Gallia ad septentriones vergit, maturae sunt hiemes,
> tamen in Britanniam proficisci contendit, quod omnibus fere
> Gallicis bellis hostibus nostris inde sumministrata auxilia
> intellegebat et, si tempus anni ad bellum gerendum deficeret,   5
> tamen magno sibi usui fore arbitrabatur, si modo insulam
> adisset et genus hominum perspexisset, loca, portus, aditus
> cognovisset; quae omnia fere Gallis erant incognita. Neque
> enim temere praeter mercatores illo adiit quisquam neque eis
> ipsis quicquam praeter oram maritimam atque eas regiones   10
> quae sunt contra Gallias notum est. Itaque vocatis ad se
> undique   mercatoribus,   neque   quanta   esset   insulae
> magnitudo, neque quae aut quantae nationes incolerent,
> neque quem usum belli haberent aut quibus institutis
> uterentur, neque   qui   essent   ad   maiorum   navium   15
> multitudinem idonei portus reperire poterat.

IV.20

exiguus, -a, -um : small, scanty
aestas, -atis (f) : summer
etsi : although
septentriones, -um (m pl) : north; the seven stars of the Great Bear (or
    Little Bear) Constellation
vergo, -ere : lie, incline
maturus, -a, -um : early; ripe
hiems, -is (f) : winter; stormy weather
Britannia, -ae (f) : Britain
sumministro (1) : provide, supply (with *sumministrata* understand *esse*)
5 *deficio, -ficere, -feci, -fectum* : be deficient, fail
magno sibi usui : translate 'of great advantage to him' (for the use of the
    dative see under *usus*, III.14)
fore : an alternative for *futurum esse*, the future infinitive of *sum*
modo : only, merely, just
adeo, -ire, -ii (or -ivi), -itum : go to, approach
perspicio, -spicere, -spexi, -spectum : observe, perceive, see
loca : this form, which is neuter plural, is used to denote places
    connected with one another, i.e. a region
portus, -us (m) : harbor, port
aditus, -us (m) : approach; access
incognitus, -a, -um : unknown
temere : without cause, idly, by chance
illo : to that place, there
10 *ora, -ae (f)* : shore, coast
maritimus, -a, -um : of the sea, maritime
contra Galliam : translate 'facing Gaul'
notus, -a, -um : known, well-known
quantus, -a, -um : how great, how much (the clauses introduced by
    neque are all indirect questions depending on *reperire*)
natio, -onis (f) : tribe, race, people
15 *qui* : interrogative adjective modifying *portus*
idoneus, -a, -um : suitable, proper

IV.33 The war chariots of the Britons

At the time of Caesar's campaigns the Gauls no longer used war chariots. Accordingly he and his men encountered them for the first time in Britain. The Britons were so dexterous in chariot warfare that their tactics caused consternation among the Roman troops. A leading scholar of Celtic civilization describes the Celtic chariot in this way: "Two-wheeled, strong in structure, pared down to the minimum it was, in trained hands, quite lethal".[6]

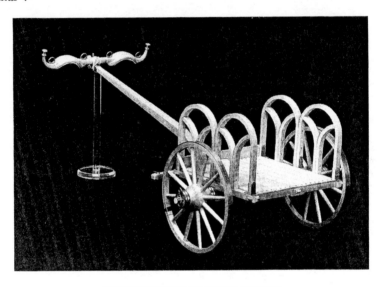

RECONSTRUCTION OF CELTIC CHARIOT
This model, which is based on a large hoard of chariot fittings from the 1st. century A.D. found in a bog in Anglesea, is in the National Museum of Wales in Cardiff.

Genus hoc est ex essedis pugnae. Primo per omnes partes perequitant et tela coiciunt atque ipso terrore equorum et strepitu rotarum ordines plerumque perturbant et, cum se inter equitum turmas insinuaverunt, ex essedis desiliunt et pedibus proeliantur. Aurigae interim paulatim ex proelio   5
excedunt atque ita currus collocant ut, si illi a multitudine hostium premantur, expeditum ad suos receptum habeant. Ita mobilitatem equitum, stabilitatem peditum in proeliis praestant, ac tantum usu cotidiano et exercitatione efficiunt uti in declivi ac praecipiti loco incitatos equos sustinere et   10
brevi moderari ac flectere et per temonem percurrere et in iugo insistere et se inde in currus citissime recipere consuerint.

IV.33

essedum, -i (n) : two-wheeled chariot (of the Gauls and Britons - the
    word is Celtic in origin)

perequito (1) : ride about

coicio, -icere, -ieci, -iectum (also spelt *-con*) : hurl, fling; infer,
    conjecture

terrore equorum : i.e. the terror inspired *by* the horses

strepitus, -us (m) : din, noise

rota, -ae (f) : wheel

ordo, -inis (f) : rank (of soldiers); row, line; order

*plerumque : generally

perturbo (1) : throw into confusion

*eques, -itis (m) : cavalryman, horseman, knight

turma, -ae (f) : squadron, troop

insinuo (1) : work one's way into, penetrate

desilio, -silire, -silui : jump down

proelior, -ari, -atus sum : fight, join battle

auriga, -ae (c) : driver, charioteer

interim : meanwhile

paulatim : gradually

currus, -us (m) : chariot

illi : i.e. the men who had alighted from the chariots

*premo, -ere, pressi, pressum : press, oppress

expeditus, -a, -um : ready to hand; unobstructed

ad suos : translate 'to their own lines'

receptus, -us (m) : retreat, withdrawal

mobilitas, -atis (f) : mobility, quickness

stabilitas, -atis (f) : stability, firmness; durability

tantum...efficiunt : translate 'they achieve such expertise'

uti : *ut*, to be taken with *consuerint*

declivis, -e : steep, sloping downwards

praeceps, -cipitis : precipitous, suddenly descending; headlong

incitatos equos sustinere : translate 'to check their horses at the gallop'
    (sustinere and the infinitives that follow are dependent on
    consuerint)

brevi : in a moment, quickly

moderor, -ari, -atus sum : restrain, check, control

flecto, -ere, flexi, flexum : turn, bend

temo, -onis (m) : chariot pole; pole, beam

percurro, -currere, -cucurri (or *-curri), -cursum* : run along, run over,
    run through

insisto, -sistere, -stiti : stand on; pursue

citissime : very quickly (superlative of the adverb *cito*)

*consuesco, -suescere, -suevi, -suetum : become accustomed
    (consuerint = consueverint)

Footnotes for Book IV :

1. For a discussion see J.P.V.D. Balsdon, 'The Veracity of Caesar', *Greece and Rome* (1957), pp.26-7.

2. *B.C.,* I.9,2

3. A. & P. Wiseman, op. cit., p.79

4. Again Caesar would be campaigning outside of his provinces; C.E. Stevens has pointed out that the invasion was as much a reconnaissance of public opinion as anything; see *Antiquity*, XXI (1947), pp.3ff.

5. S.A. Handford & J.F. Gardner, op. cit., p.231

6. B. Cunliffe, *The Celtic World* (1979), p.54

BOOK V

The second invasion of Britain

In 54 B.C. Caesar sailed to Britain with five legions and two thousand cavalry in a huge fleet that totalled eight hundred ships. His object must have been to annex at least part of the island as a Roman province. However, the guerrilla tactics of king Cassivellaunus, who led the southeastern Britons, while not sufficient to defeat the Romans certainly tested them, and a quick conquest of the island proved impossible. After a stay of two to three months Caesar, anticipating rebellion in Gaul, decided to recross the channel before winter set in, which he did after receiving hostages and imposing an annual tribute. It was not until the invasion of the emperor Claudius in 43 A.D. that any part of Britain was annexed to Rome.

The passages in which Caesar describes the geography of Britain and its inhabitants are among the best known of his writings.

V.12 The inhabitants and resources of Britain

The information that Caesar gives in this passage is on the whole accurate.

He is correct in his reference to a Belgic migration to Britain. This occurred in the second century B.C. with the first settlers arriving possibly as early as 150 B.C.[1] The first Celtic migrations to Britain had taken place hundreds of years earlier, in the eighth or seventh centuries B.C.[2]

Caesar's comment regarding density of population may well be borne out by a recent study that suggests a population increase in Britain from around 10,000 in the third millennium B.C. to a million or more at the end of the first.[3]

More than 1,500 iron bars have been found which may be identified with the bars that Caesar says were used for currency. Most of these are unfinished swords.[4]

He is correct in saying that tin and iron were found in Britain, although the tin, which was mined in Cornwall, could not have come from an inland area as he says. He writes that the Britons used *aere importato*. *Aes* can mean copper or bronze (or money), but from the context it is clear that in the phrase *aere importato* copper is meant. Copper is found in

47

Britain, but it does not appear to have been mined before the Roman occupation. Therefore it is likely that it was indeed imported at this time for use in the bronze foundries that certainly existed.[5]

Contrary to what he says, the beech tree was growing there in his day, if beech is what he means by *fagus*.

He notes that it was sacrilege to eat hares, fowl and geese. The fact that these animals appear frequently in Celtic religious art lends weight to his observation.[6]

> Britanniae pars interior ab eis incolitur quos natos in insula ipsi memoria proditum dicunt, maritima pars ab eis qui praedae ac belli inferendi causa ex Belgio transierant, qui omnes fere eis nominibus civitatum appellantur quibus orti ex civitatibus eo pervenerunt, et bello inlato ibi   5
> permanserunt atque agros colere coeperunt. Hominum est infinita multitudo creberrimaque aedificia fere Gallicis consimilia, pecorum magnus numerus. Utuntur aut aere aut nummo aureo aut taleis ferreis ad certum pondus examinatis pro nummo. Nascitur ibi plumbum album in mediterraneis   10
> regionibus, in maritimis ferrum, sed eius exigua est copia; aere utuntur importato. Materia cuiusque generis ut in Gallia est, praeter fagum atque abietem. Leporem et gallinam et anserem gustare fas non putant; haec tamen alunt animi voluptatisque causa. Loca sunt temperatiora quam in Gallia,   15
> remissioribus frigoribus.

V.12
interior, -ius : interior, inner
nascor, nasci, natus sum : be born, arise; be found; originate (with *natos* understand *esse*)
prodo, -dere, -didi, -ditum : hand down; make known; betray (with *proditum* understand *esse*)
quos...dicunt : quos...natos (esse) is the subject of *proditum...* (esse); the whole expression is the object of *dicunt*; very literally 'whom they themselves say (the fact) that they originated on the island has been handed down by tradition (*memoria*)'
praeda, -ae, (f) : booty, plunder
Belgium, -i (n) : Belgium (the territory of the *Belgae*)
orior, oriri, ortus sum : arise, rise
5   civitatibus : the antecedent of the relative is repeated and should not be translated
permaneo, -manere, -mansi, -mansum : remain

colo, -ere, -ui, cultum : till, cultivate; worship

coepi, coepisse, coeptum : begin (in classical Latin the tenses of the perfect and supine stems only are used)

creber, -bra, -brum : numerous, thick

aedificium, -i (n) : building, house

consimilis, -e : identical, very like

aes, aeris (n) : bronze; copper; money; in l.8 the meaning is 'bronze'

nummus, -i (m) : coin, currency

aureus, -a, -um : made of gold, golden

talea, -ae (f) : bar; block

ferreus, -a, -um : made of iron

certus, -a, -um : fixed, certain, definite

pondus, -eris (n) : weight

examino (1) : weigh; test, examine

10 *plumbum album* : tin (*plumbum, -i (n)* = lead; *albus, -a, -um* = white)

mediterraneus, -a, -um : inland, midland

ferrum, -i (n) : iron

aere (l.12) : from the context 'copper'

cuiusque : from *quisque, quaeque, quodque* = every, each

fagus, -i (f) : beech tree

abies, -ietis (f) : fir tree

lepus, -oris (m) : hare

gallina, -ae (f) : chicken

anser, -is (m) : goose

gusto (1) : taste; enjoy

fas (n) (indeclinable noun) : right; divine law

animi voluptatisque causa : translate 'for pleasure and enjoyment'

15 *temperatus, -a, -um* : mild, temperate

remissus, -a, -um : mild, relaxed

frigus, -oris (n) : cold, cold weather

V.13 The coast of Britain

The first side of Britain that Caesar describes is the south coast, the second the west coast, and the third the northeastern seaboard that faces the Scandinavian countries. He reflects ancient geographical misconceptions in locating the western side opposite both Ireland and Spain. All three sides of Britain are shorter than he estimated them to be, but his figures are not wildly off. "But perhaps the most remarkable feature in his description was the approximate accuracy of his estimate of the size of the island."[7]

CAESAR'S GEOGRAPHY OF BRITAIN

Insula natura triquetra, cuius unum latus est contra Galliam. Huius lateris alter angulus, qui est ad Cantium, quo fere omnes ex Gallia naves appelluntur, ad orientem solem, inferior ad meridiem spectat. Hoc pertinet circiter milia passuum quingenta. Alterum vergit ad Hispaniam atque   5
occidentem solem; qua ex parte est Hibernia, dimidio minor, ut existimatur, quam Britannia, sed pari spatio transmissus atque ex Gallia est in Britanniam. In hoc medio cursu est insula quae appellatur Mona: complures praeterea minores subiectae insulae existimantur, de quibus insulis non nulli   10
scripserunt dies continuos XXX sub bruma esse noctem. Nos nihil de eo percontationibus reperiebamus nisi certis ex aqua mensuris breviores esse quam in continenti noctes videbamus. Huius est longitudo lateris, ut fert illorum opinio, septingentorum milium. Tertium est contra   15
septentriones, cui parti nulla est obiecta terra; sed eius angulus lateris maxime ad Germaniam spectat. Hoc milia passuum octingenta in longitudinem esse existimatur. Ita omnis insula est in circuitu vicies centum milium passuum.

V.13

natura : the case is ablative; translate 'by nature'

triquetrus, -a, -um : triangular

angulus, -i (m) : corner, angle

*Cantium, -i (n) : Kent; translate *ad Cantium* 'in Kent' (in addition to the
    basic meaning 'to, towards', *ad* may mean, as it does here, 'in, at,
    in the neighborhood of'

*quo : where, whither

appello, -pellere, -puli, -pulsum : drive to land (of a ship); drive to,
    bring to

*sol, -is (m) : sun; translate *orientem solem* 'the east'

inferior : understand *angulus*

meridies, -ei (m) : south; midday

hoc : understand *latus*

circiter : about, approximately

5 *quingenti, -ae, -a* : five hundred

alterum : understand *latus*

Hispania, -ae (f) : Spain

occidens, -entis : setting; translate *occidentem solem* 'the west'

qua ex parte : translate 'on this side'

Hibernia, -ae (f) : Ireland

dimidium, -i (n) : half

minor, -us : smaller, less; *dimidio minor* - literally 'smaller by half'

transmissus, -us (m) : crossing, passage

atque : as (in conjunction with *pari*); *pari...atque* literally 'with an equal
    distance of passage across as'

cursus, -us (m) : journey; running; course; translate *in hoc medio cursu*
    'in the middle of this crossing'

Mona, -ae (f) : the Isle of Man

*praeterea : besides

10 *subiectus, -a, -um* : lying near, adjacent

bruma, -ae (f) : the winter solstice; winter; translate *sub bruma* 'at the
    winter solstice'

percontatio, -onis (f) : enquiry, searching

ex aqua : translate 'with a water-clock'

mensura, -ae (f) : measurement

brevis, -e : short

continens, -entis (f) : continent, mainland

ut fert illorum opinio : translate 'in the opinion of the Britons'

15 *septingenti, -ae, -a* : seven hundred

milium : understand *passuum*

tertium : understand *latus*

obiectus, -a, -um : opposite, lying in the way

octingenti, -ae, -a : eight hundred

circuitus, -us (m) : circumference, way round; circuit

vicies : twenty times

V.14 The inhabitants of Kent and of the interior

Caesar paints a picture of the British, with the exception of the people of Kent, as backward barbarians. His assertion that the inhabitants of the interior were not agriculturalists is contradicted by several scholars. One notes that Britain at this time was "a nation of farmers".[8] Another observes: "Throughout Britain the people lived mainly in agricultural tribal communities, sometimes centered around a hill-fortress. They were a stable and industrious population, tilling the soil and keeping livestock".[9]

His picture of the people is further contradicted by archaeological evidence of their handicraft. Examples of jewelry, pottery, weapons and tools from widespread sites attest to high standards of Celtic craftsmanship in Britain at this time.[10]

Caesar's remarks about groups of ten and twelve men sharing wives are puzzling since polyandry is not elsewhere attested for any of the Celts. Possibly the practice existed in some remote parts of Britain, and this was reported to Caesar.[11]

Ex eis omnibus longe sunt humanissimi qui Cantium incolunt, quae regio est maritima omnis, neque multum a Gallica differunt consuetudine. Interiores plerique frumenta non serunt, sed lacte et carne vivunt pellibusque sunt vestiti. Omnes vero se Britanni vitro inficiunt, quod caeruleum   5 efficit colorem, atque hoc horridiores sunt in pugna aspectu; capilloque sunt promisso atque omni parte corporis rasa, praeter caput et labrum superius. Uxores habent deni duodenique inter se communes, et maxime fratres cum fratribus parentesque cum liberis; sed qui sunt ex eis nati   10 eorum habentur liberi quo primum virgo quaeque deducta est.

V.14

Before you read this passage review the vocabulary list of IV.1. Many words are repeated here.

humanus, -a, -um : civilized; human
interiores : translate 'the inhabitants of the interior'
plerusque, -aque, -umque : most, the greater part
sero, -ere, sevi, satum : sow, plant
caro, carnis (f) : flesh
vestio, -ire, -ivi, -itum : clothe
5 *vero* : indeed, truly
vitrum, -i (n) : woad (a plant producing a blue dye); glass
inficio, -ficere, -feci, -fectum : stain, dye
caeruleus, -a, -um : blue
hoc : ablative of cause; translate 'because of this'
horridus, -a, -um : wild, frightful
aspectus, -us (m) : appearance; translate *aspectu* 'in appearance'
capillus, -i (m) : hair (the ablative *capillo...promisso* is descriptive; so too *omni parte...rasa*)
promitto, -mittere, -misi, -missum : let grow (of hair); promise
rado, -ere, rasi, rasum : shave, scrape, erase
caput, -itis (n) : head
labrum, -i (n) : lip, edge
uxor, -oris (f) : wife
deni, -ae, -a : ten at a time
duodeni, -ae, -a : twelve at a time
communis, -e : shared, common
10 *habentur* : translate 'are considered'; in addition to the basic meaning 'have' or 'hold' *habeo* also commonly bears the meaning 'consider' (be alert for several occurrences in the next passage)
virgo, -inis (f) : maiden, virgin
quo : to whom
deduco, -ducere, -duxi, -ductum : lead off; lead down

Footnotes for Book V :

1. S. Frere, *Britannia: A History of Roman Britain* (1987), p.10

2. L. Laing, *Celtic Britain* (1979), p.9; see also *Oxford Classical Dictionary* (1978), s.v. 'Celts'

3. P.J. Fowler, *The Farming of Prehistoric Britain* (1983), pp.32ff.

4. L. Laing, op. cit., p.45; G. Webster, *The Roman Invasion of Britain* (1980), p.41

5. See D.A.S. John, *Caesar's Expeditions to Britain* (1987), p.58 and R.C. Carrington, *Caesar, De Bello Gallico V* (1984), pp.86-7.

6. L. Laing, op. cit., p.39

7. T. Rice Holmes, *Ancient Britain and the Invasions of Julius Caesar* (1907), p.352

8. L. Laing, op. cit., p.37

9. P.B. Ellis, *Caesar's Invasion of Britain* (1978), p.46; cf. Fowler, op. cit., p.60 on Britain in the first millennium B.C.: "Arable field systems have been plotted over many thousands of square kilometres, and it is now generally appreciated that even this extent is but a small fraction of the land that was under cultivation, periodically or otherwise during these centuries".

10. See e.g. Laing, op. cit., pp.33-35 and pp.41ff.; Ellis, op. cit., pp.50ff.

11. T. Rice Holmes, op. cit., pp.351-2

BOOK VI

Caesar's Gallo-German Ethnography

The sixth year of campaigning (53 B.C.) saw Caesar check a number of revolts in northern Gaul and conquer the Menapii, the only tribe that had never submitted to the Romans. Meanwhile his general Titus Atius Labienus defeated the Treveri. Caesar then recrossed the Rhine and forced the retreat of the Suebi. At the point in his *Commentaries* where he returned to the Gallic bank of the Rhine, Caesar inserted his famous Gallo-German ethnography (VI.11-28).

Some scholars have questioned the authenticity of these passages and have argued that they (along with the passages of a similar nature about the Britons and the Suebi) were not written by Caesar but were later interpolations. However, this view has now been generally abandoned, and there is no good reason to doubt that they are authentic.[1]

(The sections of VI.11-28 that are not for translation in this book are given in English in Appendix A)

VI.13 & 14 Caesar's account of the druids

Druidism had long been established in Gaul by the time of Caesar's invasion, and it was natural that he would include it in his account of the customs of the Gauls.

He errs in distinguishing the druids as the only class of intellectuals in Gaul. Two other ancient writers, Diodorus Siculus and Strabo, both mention bards and augurers in addition to druids.[2] "An occasional overlap in function may have obscured the differences and led Caesar into his somewhat inaccurate generalization."[3]

Caesar records the belief that druidism originated in Britain, but this is not accepted as a certainty. Possibly it flourished more vigorously in Britain in his day, and this is what lies behind his statement.[4] There is the possibility of Greek influence in druidism by way of the Greek colony Massilia (modern Marseilles). We note Caesar's remarks about the Greek alphabet and the belief in the immortality of the soul, which brings to mind Pythagoras.[5]

In omni Gallia eorum hominum qui aliquo sunt numero
atque honore genera sunt duo. Nam plebes paene servorum
habetur loco, quae nihil audet per se, nullo adhibetur
consilio. Plerique, cum aut aere alieno aut magnitudine
tributorum aut iniuria potentiorum premuntur, sese in   5
servitutem dicant nobilibus, quibus in hos eadem omnia sunt
iura quae dominis in servos. Sed de his duobus generibus
alterum est druidum, alterum equitum. Illi rebus divinis
intersunt, sacrificia publica ac privata procurant, religiones
interpretantur: ad hos magnus adulescentium numerus   10
disciplinae causa concurrit, magnoque hi sunt apud eos
honore. Nam fere de omnibus controversiis publicis
privatisque constituunt et, si quod est admissum facinus, si
caedes facta, si de hereditate, de finibus controversia est,
idem decernunt, praemia poenasque constituunt; si qui aut   15
privatus aut populus eorum decreto non stetit, sacrificiis
interdicunt. Haec poena apud eos est gravissima. Quibus ita
est interdictum, hi numero impiorum ac sceleratorum
habentur, his omnes decedunt, aditum sermonemque
defugiunt, ne quid ex contagione incommodi accipiant,   20
neque his petentibus ius redditur, neque honos ullus
communicatur. His autem omnibus druidibus praeest unus,
qui summam inter eos habet auctoritatem. Hoc mortuo, aut
si qui ex reliquis excellit dignitate succedit, aut, si sunt
plures pares, suffragio druidum, non numquam etiam armis   25
de principatu contendunt. Hi certo anni tempore in finibus
Carnutum, quae regio totius Galliae media habetur,
considunt in loco consecrato. Huc omnes undique qui
controversias habent conveniunt eorumque decretis
iudiciisque parent. Disciplina in Britannia reperta atque inde   30
in Galliam translata esse existimatur, et nunc qui diligentius
eam rem cognoscere volunt plerumque illo discendi causa
proficiscuntur.

VI.13

aliqui, aliqua, aliquod : some; *aliquo…numero* translate 'of some
     account'

plebes (also plebs), plebis (f) : common people, plebeians

audeo, -ere, ausus sum : dare (a semi-deponent verb)

per se : translate 'on their own initiative'

adhibeo, -hibere, -hibui, -hibitum : summon, invite; apply

consilium, -i (n) : council; plan; counsel

aes alienum : debt

tributum, -i (n) : tax; tribute

potens, -entis : powerful

dico (1) : give up; devote, dedicate

quibus : dative of possession (so too *dominis*)

in hos : translate 'over them'

druides, -um (m pl) : druids

equitum : Caesar is referring to the Gallic nobility

intersum, -esse, -fui : take part in (with dative); be between

procuro (1) : attend to, take care of

religiones : translate 'religious matters'

interpretor, -pretari, -pretatus sum : explain

concurro, -currere, -curri, -cursum : run eagerly; run together; meet in
     battle

honos, honoris (m) : honor, glory

controversia, -ae (f) : dispute, lawsuit; debate

si quod : if any (to be taken with *facinus*)

admitto, -mittere, -misi, -missum : commit; admit

facinus, -oris (n) : crime; deed

caedes, -is (f) : murder, slaughter

facta : understand *est*

hereditas, -atis (f) : inheritance

decerno, -cernere, -crevi, -cretum : decide, resolve

praemium, -i (n) : reward, prize

poena, -ae (f) : punishment, penalty

si qui aut privatus aut populus : translate 'if either any individual or
     community'

decretum, -i (n) : decision, resolution; translate *eorum decreto non stetit*
     'has not stood by their decision'

sacrificiis : ablative of separation - 'from sacrifices'

interdico, -dicere, -dixi, -dictum : forbid, prohibit (with dative of
     person - *quibus* in l.17 with *est interdictum* is such a dative)

impius, -a, -um : impious, undutiful

sceleratus, -a, -um : accursed, polluted, criminal, villainous

decedo, -cedere, -cessi, -cessum : withdraw, retire (with dative of person
     his); translate *his…decedunt* 'shun them'

sermo, -onis (m) : conversation, speech

20 *defugio, -fugere, -fugi* : avoid, run away from
quid : anything (following *ne*)
contagio, -onis (f) : contact; contagion
incommodum, -i (n) : misfortune, inconvenience (*incommodi* is a partitive
      genitive following *quid*)
petentibus : *peto* is here used in the legal sense of 'bringing a suit'
reddo, reddere, reddidi, redditum : render; give in return; give back,
      restore
communico (1) : share
praesum, -esse, -fui : be in charge (with dative)
morior, mori, mortuus sum : die
excello, -cellere : stand out, excel
dignitas, -atis (f) : dignity; worth
succedo, -cedere, -cessi, -cessum : succeed, come after; come up
25 *plures, -a* (genitive *plurium*) : several, many
suffragium, -i (n) : vote
non numquam : sometimes (also written as one word)
principatus, -us (m) : the first place, chief command; rule or sovereignty
      (of the emperor)
Carnutes, -um (m pl) : the Carnutes (a tribe of Central Gaul)
consido, -sidere, -sedi : sit in session; sit down; encamp
consecratus, -a, -um : holy, consecrated
huc : here, to this place
30 *iudicium, -i (n)* : judgment, decision; court; trial
pareo, -ere, -ui, -itum : obey (with dative)
diligentius : the form is the comparative degree of the adverb
disco, -ere, didici : learn

Strabo on the Bards, Vates and Druids of the Gauls

Among all the Gauls generally speaking there are three classes of men who are especially honored: the Bards, the Vates and the Druids. The Bards are singers and poets; the Vates are augurers and natural philosophers; while the Druids, in addition to natural philosophy, also study moral philosophy. The Druids are considered to be exceptionally just and because of this they are entrusted with the decision of both private and public cases; in fact in former times they arbitrated wars and stopped the combatants when they were about to take up position for battle; and murder cases especially have been turned over to them for decision. When there is a good yield of victims from these cases, they believe that this leads to a good yield from the fields. The Druids and others too say that individual souls and the universe are indestructible, although both fire and water may at some time prevail over them. (Strabo, IV.4,4)

VI.14

Druides a bello abesse consuerunt, neque tributa una cum
reliquis pendunt; militiae vacationem omniumque rerum
habent immunitatem. Tantis excitati praemiis et sua sponte
multi   in   disciplinam   conveniunt   et   a   parentibus
propinquisque mittuntur. Magnum ibi numerum versuum   5
ediscere dicuntur. Itaque annos non nulli XX in disciplina
permanent. Neque fas esse existimant ea litteris mandare,
cum in reliquis fere rebus, publicis privatisque rationibus,
Graecis litteris utantur. Id mihi duabus de causis instituisse
videntur, quod neque in vulgum disciplinam efferri velint   10
neque eos qui discunt litteris confisos minus memoriae
studere; quod fere plerisque accidit ut praesidio litterarum
diligentiam in perdiscendo ac memoriam remittant. In primis
hoc volunt persuadere, non interire animas sed ab aliis post
mortem transire ad alios, atque hoc maxime ad virtutem   15
excitari putant, metu mortis neglecto. Multa praeterea de
sideribus   atque   eorum   motu,   de   mundi   ac   terrarum
magnitudine, de rerum natura, de deorum immortalium vi ac
potestate disputant et iuventuti tradunt.

VI.14

consuerunt : for *consueverunt*
una cum : together with
pendo, -ere, pependi, pensum : pay; weigh out
militia, -ae (f) : military service, warfare; the military
vacatio, -onis (f) : exemption, freedom
immunitas, -atis (f) : freedom from taxes or public services; immunity,
        exemption
5   *excito (1)* : rouse, awaken, stir; translate *excitati* 'attracted'
    propinquus, -i (m) : relative, kinsman
    edisco, -discere, -didici : learn by heart
    littera, -ae (f) : letter (of alphabet); in plural 'letter, epistle; literature;
        documents'
    mando (1) : entrust; command
    cum : although
    rationibus : here 'accounts'
    Graecis litteris : Caesar means that in secular affairs they write their own
        language with the Greek alphabet
10 *videntur* : the passive of *video* often means 'seem'
    vulgus, -i (n) : common people; crowd
    effero, -ferre, extuli, elatum : make known, publish; carry out

eos : object, along with *disciplinam*, of *velint*
confido, -fidere, -fisus sum : rely on, trust (with dative)
minus...studere : translate 'to give less attention to'
accido, -cidere, -cidi : happen; fall at or near
praesidium, -i (n) : help; protection; garrison
perdisco, -discere, -didici : learn thoroughly
remitto, -mittere, -misi, -missum : let go, relax; send back
in primis : especially (also written *imprimis*)
hoc persuadere : translate 'to persuade people of this' (*hoc* is explained
    by the accusative and infinitive construction that follows)
intereo, -ire, -ii, -itum : perish, pass away
anima, -ae (f) : soul, spirit
15   *hoc* : ablative of cause; translate 'through this belief'
excitari : translate 'that men are aroused'
metus, -us (m) : fear
neglego, -legere, -lexi, -lectum : neglect, disregard
sidus, -eris (n) : heavenly body, constellation
motus, -us (m) : movement; uprising; emotion
mundus, -i (m) : universe, world
rerum natura : translate 'the nature of the physical world'
*potestas, -atis (f) : power
disputo (1) : discuss; debate, argue
iuventus, -utis (f) : young men; youth, the prime of life
trado, -dere, -didi, -ditum : hand over, hand down

VI.15 The Gallic knights

The *equites* to whom Caesar refers in this passage are the Gallic nobility. Caesar had mentioned oppressed common people (*plebes*) in VI.13 without making any distinction of free and unfree among them, an omission that may have been due to the lack of importance of these people to him in his campaigns. It is likely that the clients and retainers of the *equites* mentioned here were free peasant farmers below whom existed a class of unfree servants.[6] The following diagram may be used to illustrate the structure of Celtic society.

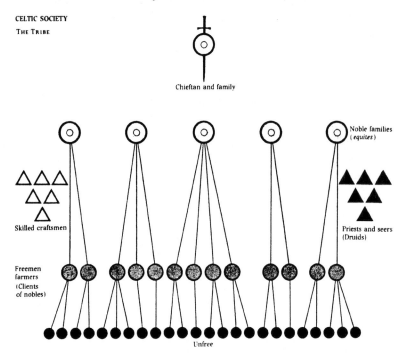

Alterum genus est equitum. Hi, cum est usus atque aliquod bellum incidit (quod fere ante Caesaris adventum quot annis accidere solebat, uti aut ipsi iniurias inferrent aut inlatas propulsarent), omnes in bello versantur; atque eorum ut quisque est genere copiisque amplissimus, ita plurimos   5
circum se ambactos clientesque habet. Hanc unam gratiam potentiamque noverunt.

VI.15

usus : here means 'need'

incido, -cidere, -cidi, -casum : happen, occur; fall in or on

quod : relative pronoun, subject of *solebat*

soleo, -ere, solitus sum : be accustomed

uti : *ut*

iniurias inferrent : translate 'were inflicting injuries'

inlatas : understand *iniurias*

propulso (1) : fend off, drive back

*versor, -ari, -atus sum : be involved in

ut : as (with indicative)

genere copiisque : ablatives of respect; translate 'in birth and wealth'

amplissimus : very important, distinguished (superlative of
         amplus, -a, -um)

ambactus, -i (m) : retainer, dependant

cliens, clientis (m) : client

hanc unam gratiam potentiamque : translate 'this one kind of influence
         and power'

nosco, -ere, novi, notum : recognize; get to know; in tenses of the perfect
         stem, as here, = 'know'

VI.16 Human sacrifices of the Gauls

Caesar's mention of the Gallic custom of human sacrifice undoubtedly fulfilled a propaganda purpose of portraying the Gauls as savage barbarians, but there is no question that it was widely practised in Gaul. It is mentioned by several other ancient writers including Diodorus Siculus, who also associates it with augury: "They devote to death a human being and stab him with a dagger in the region above the diaphragm, and when he has fallen they foretell the future from his fall and from the convulsions of his limbs, and moreover from the spurting of the blood, placing their trust in some ancient and long-continued observation of these practices".[7]

The wickerwork constructions mentioned by Caesar are also referred to by Strabo.[8]

> Natio est omnium Gallorum admodum dedita religionibus,
> atque ob eam causam qui sunt adfecti gravioribus morbis
> quique in proeliis periculisque versantur aut pro victimis
> homines immolant aut se immolaturos vovent,
> administrisque ad ea sacrificia druidibus utuntur; quod, pro   5
> vita hominis nisi hominis vita reddatur, non posse deorum
> immortalium numen placari arbitrantur, publiceque eiusdem
> generis habent instituta sacrificia. Alii immani magnitudine
> simulacra habent, quorum contexta viminibus membra vivis
> hominibus complent; quibus succensis circumventi flamma   10
> exanimantur homines. Supplicia eorum qui in furto aut in
> latrocinio aut aliqua noxia sint comprehensi gratiora dis
> immortalibus esse arbitrantur, sed, cum eius generis copia
> deficit, etiam ad innocentium supplicia descendunt.

VI.16

admodum : completely

dedo, dedere, dedidi, deditum : devote; give up

morbus, -i (m) : disease

pro victimis : translate 'as victims'

immolo (1) : sacrifice (with *immolaturos* understand *esse*)

voveo, -ere, vovi, votum : vow, promise solemnly

administer, -tri (m) : assistant, attendant

numen, -inis (n) : divine will, divinity

placo (1) : appease, calm

publice : translate 'for the community'

immani magnitudine : ablative of description

simulacrum, -i (n) : image, likeness (*simulacra* is the antecedent of the
    relative *quorum*)

contexta : translate 'woven' (it modifies *membra*)

vimen, -inis (n) : twig, shoot

membrum, -i (n) : limb; member (*membra* is accusative, object of
    complent)

vivus, -a, -um : living, alive

10   **compleo, -ere, -evi, -etum* : fill; complete

succendo, -cendere, -cendi, -censum : set on fire

circumvenio, -venire, -veni, -ventum : surround, encompass

exanimo (1) : kill; deprive of breath

supplicium, -i (n) : execution; punishment; torture (*supplicia* 1.11 is the
    accusative of an accusative and infinitive construction dependent on
    arbitrantur)

furtum, -i (n) : theft; trick, stratagem

latrocinium, -i (n) : robbery, brigandage

noxia, -ae (f) : crime, wrongdoing

sint comprehensi : subjunctive because *qui...sint comprehensi* is a
    subordinate clause in indirect speech

gratus, -a, -um : pleasing, agreeable (*gratiora* is in agreement with
    supplicia 1.11)

dis : for *deis*

VI.21 Description of the Germans

Caesar follows his description of the Gauls with one of the Germans, again emphasizing their barbaric nature.

In Caesar's time it was common to regard all the tribes from across the Rhine as Germans.[9] In reality the Rhine cannot have represented an absolute division between Celts and Germans. "It is more realistic to assume that a broad band of hybridization extended on both sides of the river."[10] In fact Caesar himself says that the Belgae were descended from Germanic tribes that had earlier crossed the Rhine.[11]

The Roman historian Tacitus says that the Germans worshipped Mercury, Hercules and Mars,[12] divinities not mentioned by Caesar here, but is in agreement with Caesar about the value attached to chastity: *sera iuvenum venus, eoque inexhausta pubertas. nec virgines festinantur*: "Love comes late for young men, and their virility is therefore not exhausted; nor are young women hurried into marriage".[13]

> Germani multum ab hac consuetudine differunt. Nam neque druides habent qui rebus divinis praesint neque sacrificiis student. Deorum numero eos solos ducunt quos cernunt et quorum aperte opibus iuvantur, Solem et Vulcanum et Lunam; reliquos ne fama quidem acceperunt. Vita omnis in   5
> venationibus atque in studiis rei militaris consistit: ab parvulis labori ac duritiae student. Qui diutissime impuberes permanserunt, maximam inter suos ferunt laudem: hoc alii staturam, alii vires nervosque confirmari putant. Intra annum vero vicesimum feminae notitiam habuisse in   10
> turpissimis habent rebus; cuius rei nulla est occultatio, quod et promiscue in fluminibus perluuntur et pellibus aut parvis renonum tegimentis utuntur magna corporis parte nuda.

VI.21

qui...praesint : translate 'to be in charge of' (a relative clause of purpose)

solus, -a, -um : only, alone

ducunt : here means 'consider'

cerno, -ere, crevi, cretum : see, discern, distinguish

aperte : openly (adverb from *apertus, -a, -um*)

ops, opis (f) : power; help; in pl. 'resources, means'

iuvo, -are, iuvi, iutum : help, assist

Vulcanus, -i (m) : Vulcan (the god of fire)

Luna, -ae (f) : Moon

ne...quidem : not even

fama, -ae (f) : common talk, rumor; reputation, fame

acceperunt : translate 'have heard'

studium, -i (n) : pursuit; enthusiasm, zeal; study

rei militaris : translate 'warfare'

consistit : translate 'consists of' (*consisto* with *in* + ablative bears this
        meaning)

ab parvulis : translate 'from childhood'

duritia, -ae (f) : hardship, austerity; hardness

diutissime : for the longest time (superlative adverb from *diu*)

impubes, -beris : celibate; youthful

laus, laudis (f) : praise

hoc : ablative; translate 'through this', i.e. through chastity or celibacy

statura, -ae (f) : stature, size

nervus, -i (m) : muscle, sinew; nerve; thong; bowstring

intra : inside, within (preposition with accusative); here translate 'before'

vicesimus, -a, -um: twentieth

notitia, -ae (f) : knowledge, acquaintance; here translate 'intercourse'

turpis, -e : disgraceful, shameful; ugly

habent : translate 'they consider'

cuius rei : translate 'of sexual matters'

occultatio, -onis (f) : hiding, concealment

promiscue : together, in common; promiscuously

perluo, -luere, -lui, -lutum : bathe, wash completely; the passive is used
        as a middle here = 'bathe oneself'

reno, -onis (m) : fur

tegimentum, -i (n) : covering

VI.26 & 27 Strange animals of Germany

The creature mentioned by Caesar in VI.26 must be the reindeer, although in reality, of course, it has two horns. Caesar seems excessively gullible in VI.27 in giving credence to what he was told about the elk.

VI.26

Est bos cervi figura, cuius a media fronte inter aures unum cornu exsistit excelsius magisque directum eis quae nobis nota sunt cornibus. Ab eius summo sicut palmae ramique late diffunduntur. Eadem est feminae marisque natura, eadem forma magnitudoque cornuum.   5

VI.27

Sunt item quae appellantur alces. Harum est consimilis capris figura et varietas pellium, sed magnitudine paulo antecedunt, mutilaeque sunt cornibus, et crura sine nodis articlisque habent, neque quietis causa procumbunt neque, si quo adflictae casu conciderunt, erigere sese aut sublevare   5 possunt. His sunt arbores pro cubilibus: ad eas se applicant atque ita paulum modo reclinatae quietem capiunt. Quarum ex vestigiis cum est animadversum a venatoribus quo se recipere consuerint, omnes eo loco aut ab radicibus subruunt aut accidunt arbores, tantum ut summa species earum   10 stantium relinquatur. Huc cum se consuetudine reclinaverunt, infirmas arbores pondere adfligunt atque una ipsae concidunt.

VI.26

bos, bovis (m or f) : ox, bull; cow
cervus, -i (m) : stag, deer
*figura, -ae (f) : shape, figure, form; translate *figura* 'with the shape' (the
        case is ablative)
cuius a media fronte : translate 'from the middle of whose forehead'
auris, -is (f) : ear
exsisto, -sistere, -stiti, -stitum : stand forth, appear; come into existence
excelsius : higher (comparative from *excelsus, -a, -um*)
magis : more
directus, -a, -um : straight
eis...cornibus : ablative of comparison
summum, -i (n) : top
sicut : as it were; just as

palma, -ae (f) : hand, palm of the hand; palm tree, palm branch
ramus, -i (m) : branch
diffundo, -fundere, -fudi, -fusum : spread out; pour out (the top of the
    antler branches out like fingers from the palm of the hand, or
    branches from a tree)
mas, maris (m) : male, man

VI.27
alces, -is (f) : elk
caper, -ri (m) : goat
varietas, -atis (f) : variety, diversity (Caesar means that the animals were
    dappled or piebald)
antecedo, -cedere, -cessi, -cessum : surpass; go before, precede
mutilus, -a, -um : stunted; maimed, mutilated
cornibus : ablative of respect
crus, cruris (n) : leg
sine nodis articlisque : translate 'without joints and knuckles'
quies, -ietis (f) : sleep, rest; quiet
procumbo, -cumbere, -cubui, -cubitum : sink to the ground; lean forward
si quo...casu : translate 'if by some accident'
5 *adfligo, -fligere, -flixi, -flictum* : knock down; damage, injure
concido, -cidere, -cidi : fall down; perish
erigo, -rigere, -rexi, -rectum : lift up; set up, erect; arouse
sublevo (1) : raise, lift
cubile, -is (n) : bed, couch
applico (1) : place near; attach
paulum modo reclinatae : translate 'leaning over very slightly'
vestigium, -i (n) : track, footstep; trace
venator, -is (m) : hunter
omnes : accusative plural with *arbores*
radix, -icis (f) : root; foundation, base
subruo, -ruere, -rui, -rutum : undermine, tear from below
10 *accido, -cidere, -cidi, -cisum* : cut at; weaken
tantum...relinquatur : literally 'so far that the complete appearance of
    them standing is left'
consuetudine : translate 'according to their habit'
reclino (1) : recline; bend back, lean back
infirmus, -a, -um : weakened, weak
una : at the same time, together

Footnotes for Book VI :

1. See F.E. Adcock, op. cit., pp.96ff. for a discussion of the veracity of the digressions; a valuable collection of primary sources on the Celts (Athenaeus, Diodorus Siculus, Strabo and Caesar) is contained in J.J. Tierney, 'The Celtic Ethnography of Posidonius', *Proceedings of the Royal Irish Academy*, vol. 60, sect. C, no. 5 (1960) (the lost writings of Posidonius about the Celts can be reconstructed from later writers who were indebted to him).

2. Diodorus, V.31,2-3; Strabo, IV.4,4

3. B. Cunliffe, op. cit., p.106

4. T. Rice Holmes, *Caesar's Conquest of Gaul* (1911), p.525

5. For an example of a scholar who sees such influence see N. Chadwick, *The Druids* (1966), p.102.

6. A. & P. Wiseman, op. cit., p.120; see also Cunliffe, op. cit., p.48; Rice Holmes, op. cit., p.515 thinks that the *ambacti* may have been "retainers of a lower grade than *clientes*".

7. Diodorus, V.31,3; translation from J.J. Tierney, op. cit., p.251

8. Strabo, IV.4,5

9. B. Cunliffe, op. cit., p.141; T.G.E. Powell, *The Celts* (1980), p.191

10. A. & P. Wiseman, op. cit., p.128; note too Powell's remark, op. cit., p.192: "there must have been a shading off of cultural, linguistic, and political affiliations from one major natural region to another".

11. *B.G.,* II.4

12. *Germania* 9

13. *Germania* 20

BOOK VII

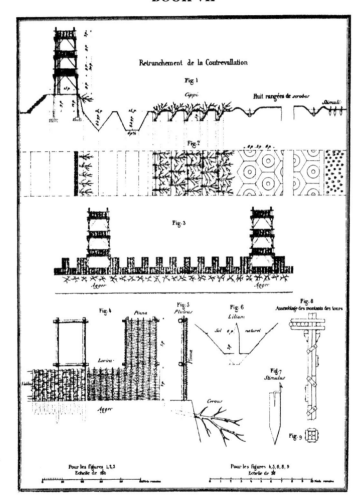

THE SIEGE OF ALESIA
(from Napoleon III's *Histoire de Jules Cesar*)

In front of the works described in the next passage for translation disguised pits were built to trap the enemy, and behind the eleven mile circumvallation yet another was built fourteen miles in circumference to protect against the relieving army. Napoleon III was so intrigued by Caesar's account of the siege of Alesia that he undertook to find the site. His collaborator, Colonel Stoffel, found it at modern Alise Ste. Reine.

71

VII.72 Vercingetorix is besieged in Alesia

Caesar had faced insurrections by Gallic tribes before, but nothing that
compared with that of the year 52 B.C. under Vercingetorix, charismatic
leader of the Arverni. With only a few exceptions all the Gallic tribes
accepted his able leadership and rose up in one last attempt to throw off
the Roman yoke.

The Romans suffered a major defeat at Gergovia where forty-six
centurions were killed, and it was at that point that the Aedui, so long
loyal allies of Rome, joined Vercingetorix. The final actions of the war
took place at Alesia, a hill-town behind whose walls Vercingetorix
withdrew his army. Caesar ultimately prevailed but only after one of the
great sieges of history.

Initially Caesar constructed eleven miles of siege-works around the town,
but when he found that Vercingetorix had sent out his cavalry to gather a
relieving force he decided that further measures were necessary.

> Quibus rebus cognitis ex perfugis et captivis, Caesar haec
> genera munitionis instituit. Fossam pedum XX derectis
> lateribus duxit, ut eius fossae solum tantundem pateret
> quantum summae fossae labra distarent. Reliquas omnes
> munitiones ab ea fossa passus quadringentos reduxit, id hoc   5
> consilio,   quoniam   tantum   esset   necessario   spatium
> complexus nec facile totum opus corona militum cingeretur,
> ne de improviso aut noctu ad munitiones hostium multitudo
> advolaret aut interdiu tela in nostros operi destinatos coicere
> possent. Hoc intermisso spatio duas fossas quindecim pedes   10
> latas   eadem   altitudine   perduxit,   quarum   interiorem
> campestribus ac demissis locis aqua ex flumine derivata
> complevit. Post eas aggerem ac vallum XII pedum exstruxit.
> Huic   loricam   pinnasque   adiecit,   grandibus   cervis
> eminentibus ad commissuras pluteorum atque aggeris qui   15
> ascensum hostium tardarent, et turres toto opere circumdedit
> quae pedes LXXX inter se distarent.

VII.72

perfuga, -ae (m) : deserter, refugee
fossa, -ae (f) : ditch, trench
derectus, -a, -um : perpendicular, straight
duxit : translate 'he dug'
solum, -i (n) : bottom; soil, ground
tantundem...quantum : translate 'to the same extent as'
summae...fossae : translate 'of the top of the ditch'
labrum, -i (n) : edge, lip
disto (1) : stand apart, be separate
quadringenti, -ae, -a : four hundred
reduco, -ducere, -duxi, -ductum : bring back, lead back
hoc consilio : is explained by the clauses *ne...advolaret* and *aut...possent*
quoniam : since, because
tantum...spatium : object of *esset...complexus* = *complexus esset*
complector, -plecti, -plexus sum : enclose; embrace; the subjunctive is
    potential - 'he would have enclosed'
corona, -ae (f) : ring, circle; crown, garland (*corona* is ablative of
    means)
cingo, -ere, cinxi, cinctum : surround, encircle; tuck up (of a garment);
    for the subjunctive see *esset...complexus* above
de improviso : unexpectedly
advolo (1) : rush against; fly to
interdiu : in the daytime
operi destinatos : translate 'tied to their work'
coicere, -icere, -ieci, -iectum (also spelt *con-*) : hurl, throw together;
    conjecture
10 *hoc intermisso spatio* : literally 'with this space left free'
perduxit : see *duxit* above
quarum interiorem : translate 'the inner one of which' (i.e. the one
    nearer Alesia)
campestribus ac demissis locis : translate 'on level and low-lying ground'
derivo (1) : divert, draw off
agger, -is (m) : rampart; heap, mound
vallum, -i (n) : palisade; entrenchment
exstruo, -struere, -struxi, -structum : build up, construct
lorica, -ae (f) : parapet; leather cuirass
pinna, -ae (f) : battlement; feather; wing
adicio, -icere, -ieci, -iectum : add; throw to
grandis, -e : large, great; grand
cervis : here refers to wooden stakes in the shape of antlers stuck into the
    ground as a protection
15 *emineo, -minere, -minui* : project, stand out
commissura, -ae (f) : juncture, joint; translate *ad commissuras* 'at the
    junctures'

pluteus, -i (m) (also *-um, -i (n)*) : parapet (Caesar means the entire
   defensive apparatus mounted on top of the *agger*; the stakes
   protruded from the point where the *agger* met the defences that
   were mounted on top of it)

qui...tardarent : relative clause of purpose

ascensus, -us (m) : ascent, climbing up

turris, -is (f) : turret, tower

toto opere : the ablative is one of place; translate 'on the whole work'

circumdo, -dare, -dedi, -datum : put around; surround

quae...distarent : a relative clause of characteristic explaining what *kind*
   or *sort* the towers were

Appendix A

Chapters from Caesar's Gallo-German Ethnography not for translation in this book (translation from S.A. Handford & J.F. Gardner, op. cit., pp.138-146)

VI.11

At this point, it seems not inappropriate to give an account of the customs of the Gauls and Germans and the differences between these peoples.

In Gaul, not only every tribe, canton, and subdivision of a canton, but almost every family, is divided into rival factions. At the head of these factions are men who are regarded by their followers as having particularly great prestige, and these have the final say on all questions that come up for judgement and in all discussions of policy. The object of this ancient custom seems to have been to ensure that all the common people should have protection against the strong; for each leader sees that no one gets the better of his supporters by force or by cunning - or, if he fails to do so, is utterly discredited.

The same principle holds good in inter-tribal politics: all the tribes are grouped in two factions.

VI.12

At the time of Caesar's arrival, these were headed respectively by the Aedui and the Sequani. As the Aedui had long enjoyed very great prestige and had many satellite tribes, the Sequani were the weaker of the two, depending on their own resources. They therefore secured the alliance of Ariovistus and his Germans, at the cost of heavy sacrifices and the promise of still further concessions [70-65 B.C.]. Then, as a result of several victories in which all the Aeduans of rank were killed, the Sequani became so much stronger than their rivals that they were able to bring over to their side a considerable part of the Aeduan dependencies, and to make the Aeduans surrender the sons of their chiefs as hostages and swear to form no hostile designs against the Sequani. They had also seized and retained a part of the Aeduan territory that lay near their own frontier and had in fact established a hegemony over the whole of Gaul. Reduced to this extremity, Diviciacus the Aeduan went to Rome to solicit aid from the Senate, but returned without success [61 B.C.].

Caesar's arrival changed the situation: the Aedui had their hostages restored to them, and not only regained their former dependencies but acquired new ones with Caesar's help, because those who became their allies found that they were better off and more equitably governed than before. In other respects, too, their influence and standing were enhanced, and the Sequani lost their supremacy. Their place was taken by the Remi; and as it was known that they stood as high in Caesar's favour as the Aedui, tribes which on account of old feuds could not be induced to join the Aedui were placing themselves under the protection of the Remi, who by taking good care of them were able to maintain the unaccustomed power that they had suddenly acquired. At this time, therefore, the position was that, while the Aedui were acknowledged to be easily ahead of all the other tribes, the Remi came next in importance.

VI.17

The god they reverence most is Mercury. They have very many images of him, and regard him as the inventor of all arts, the god who directs men upon their journeys, and their most powerful helper in trading and getting money. Next to him they reverence Apollo, Mars, Jupiter, and Minerva, about whom they have much the same ideas as other nations - that Apollo averts illness, and Minerva teaches the principles of industries and handicrafts; that Jupiter is king of the gods, and Mars the lord of war. When they have decided to fight a battle they generally vow to Mars the booty that they hope to take, and after a victory they sacrifice the captured animals and collect the rest of the spoil in one spot. Among many of the tribes, high piles of it can be seen on consecrated ground; and it is an almost unknown thing for anyone to dare, in defiance of religious law, to conceal his booty at home or to remove anything placed on the piles. Such a crime is punishable by a terrible death under torture.

VI.18

The Gauls claim all to be descended from Father Dis, declaring that this is the tradition preserved by the Druids. For this reason they measure periods of time not by days but by nights; and in celebrating birthdays, the first of the month, and new year's day, they go on the principle that the day begins at night. As regards the other usages of daily life, the chief difference between them and other peoples is that their children are not allowed to go up to their fathers in public until they are old enough for military service; they regard it as unbecoming for a son who is still a boy to stand in his father's sight in a public place.

VI.19

When a Gaul marries he adds to the dowry that his wife brings with her a portion of his own property estimated to be of equal value. A joint account is kept of the whole amount, and the profits which it earns are put aside; and when either dies, the survivor receives both shares together with the accumulated profits. Husbands have power of life and death over their wives as well as their children. When a high-born head of a family dies, his relatives assemble, and if the circumstances of his death are suspicious, they examine his widow under torture, as we examine slaves; if her guilt is established, she is consigned to the flames and put to death with the most cruel torments. Gallic funerals are splendid and costly, for a comparatively poor country. Everything that the dead man is supposed to have been fond of, including even animals, is placed upon his pyre; and not long ago there were people still alive who could remember the time when slaves and retainers known to have been beloved by their masters were burnt with them at the conclusion of the funeral rites.

VI.20

The tribes which are considered to manage their affairs best have a law that if anyone hears from a neighboring country any rumor or news that concerns the State, he is to communicate it to a magistrate without speaking of it to anyone else; for experience has shown that impulsive and ignorant persons are often frightened by false reports into subversive action, and meddle with important affairs of state. The magistrates suppress what they think it advisable to keep secret, and publish only what they deem it expedient for the people to know. The discussion of politics is forbidden except in a public assembly.

VI.22

The Germans are not agriculturalists, and live principally on milk, cheese, and meat. No one possesses any definite amount of land as private property; the magistrates and tribal chiefs annually assign a holding to clans and groups of kinsmen or others living together, fixing its size and position at their discretion, and the following year make them move on somewhere else. They give many reasons for this custom: for example, that their men may not get accustomed to living in one place, lose their warlike enthusiasm, and take up agriculture instead; that they may not be anxious to acquire large estates, and the strong be tempted to dispossess the weak; to prevent their paying too much attention to building houses that will protect them from cold and heat, or becoming too fond of money - a frequent cause of division and strife; and to keep the common people contented and quiet by letting every man see that even the most powerful are no better off than himself.

VI.23

The various tribes regard it as their greatest glory to lay waste as much as possible of the land around them and to keep it uninhabited. They hold it a proof of a people's valor to drive their neighbors from their homes, so that no one dare settle near them, and also think it gives them greater security by removing any fear of sudden invasion. When a tribe is attacked or intends to attack another, officers are chosen to conduct the campaign and invested with powers of life and death. In peacetime there is no central magistracy; the chiefs of the various districts and cantons administer justice and settle disputes among their own people. No discredit attaches to plundering raids outside the tribal frontiers; the Germans say that they serve to keep the young men in training and prevent them from getting lazy. When a chief announces in an assembly his intention of leading a raid and calls for volunteers, those who like the proposal, and approve of the man who makes it, stand up and promise their assistance amid the applause of the whole gathering; anyone who backs out afterwards is looked on as a deserter and traitor and no one will ever trust him again. To wrong a guest is impious in their eyes. They shield from injury all who come to their houses for any purpose whatever, and treat their persons as sacred; guests are welcomed to every man's home and table.

VI.24

There was a time when the Gauls were more warlike than the Germans, when they actually invaded German territory, and sent colonists across the Rhine because their own country was too small to support its large population. It was in this way that the most fertile district of Germany, in the neighborhood of the Hercynian forest (which I see was known to Eratosthenes and other Greeks, who call it Orcynia) was seized and occupied by the Volcae Tectosages, who remain there to this day and have a high reputation for fair dealing and gallantry. Nowadays, while the Germans still endure the same life of poverty and privation as before, without any change in their diet or clothing, the Gauls, through living near the Roman Province and becoming acquainted with seaborne products, are abundantly supplied with various commodities. Gradually accustomed to inferiority and defeated in many battles, they do not even pretend to compete with the Germans in bravery.

VI.25

This Hercynian forest is so wide that it takes a lightly equipped traveller nine days to cross it; this is the only way the Germans have of estimating its size, as they know nothing of measures of length. Starting from the frontiers of the Helvetii, Nemetes, and Rauraci, it runs straight along the Danube to the country of the Dacians and the Anartes. At this point it turns north-east away from the river, and in its huge length extends through the territories of many different peoples. No western German claims to have reached its eastern extremity, even after travelling for two months, or to have heard where it ends. The forest is known to contain many kinds of animals not seen elsewhere, some of which seem worthy of mention because they differ greatly from those found in other countries.

VI.28

A third species is the aurochs, an animal somewhat smaller than the elephant, with the appearance, color, and shape of a bull. They are very strong and agile, and attack every man and beast they catch sight of. The natives take great pains to trap them in pits, and kill them. This arduous sport toughens the young men and keeps them in training; and those who kill the largest number exhibit the horns in public to show what they have done, and earn high praise. It is impossible to domesticate or tame the aurochs, even if it is caught young. The horns are much larger than those of our oxen, and of quite different shape and appearance. The Germans prize them greatly: they mount the rims with silver and use them as drinking-cups at their grandest banquets.

Appendix B

List of words only given once in vocabulary lists and marked with an asterisk

absum, -esse, afui : be distant, be away
adduco, -ducere, -duxi, -ductum : lead on, induce; lead to, bring to
adficio, -ficere, -feci, -fectum : affect; afflict
aditus, -us (m) : approach; access
adventus, -us (m) : arrival
aes, aeris (n) : copper; bronze; money
aliqui, aliqua, aliquod : some
alius, -a, -ud : another, other
alo, -ere, -ui, altum : raise, nourish; support
alter, -era, -erum : the other; one (of two)
altitudo, -inis (f) : height; depth
amitto, -mittere, -misi, -missum : lose; let go
angustiae, -arum (f pl) : narrowness; difficulty
animadverto, -vertere, -verti, -versum : notice, pay attention to
animus, -i (m) : spirit; mind; soul; *in animo esse* = 'intend'
appello (1) : call
apud : among (preposition with accusative)
arbitror, -ari, -atus sum : consider, think, judge
auctoritas, -atis (f) : authority, influence
auxilium, -i (n) : help, aid
bellicosus, -a, -um : warlike, bellicose
bello (1) : wage war, fight
bellum gero, gerere, gessi, gestum : wage war
bellum infero, -ferre, -tuli, inlatum : make war on (with dative)
bini, -ae, -a : two at a time; two each
causa : for the sake of (with preceding genitive)
certiorem facio, -ere, feci, factum : inform
certus, -a, -um : fixed, certain, definite
circum : around, about
civitas, -atis (f) : state; citizenship
cognosco, -gnoscere, -gnovi, -gnitum : learn, get to know
colloco (1) : settle; position, arrange
compleo, -ere, -evi, -etum : fill; complete
complures, -ium : several

81

comprehendo, -prehendere, -prehendi, -prehensum : grasp, seize, arrest; comprehend

concedo, -cedere, -cessi, -cessum : allow, concede; withdraw

conficio, -ficere, -feci, -fectum : complete, carry through; wear out, exhaust

confirmo (1) : secure, strengthen; confirm

conor, -ari, -atus sum : try

consilium, -i (n) : council; plan; counsel

consimilis, -e : identical, very like

consisto, -sistere, -stiti, -stitum : halt, take a position; depend on; consist of (both with *in* + ablative)

conspectus, -us (m) : sight, view

constituo, -stituere, -stitui, -stitutum : decide, determine; establish

consuesco, -suescere, -suevi, -suetum : become accustomed

consuetudo, -inis (f) : custom, habit

contendo, -tendere, -tendi, -tentum : fight, contend; hurry; strain

contra : against; facing (preposition with accusative)

convenio, -venire, -veni, -ventum : assemble, meet, come together; agree

copia, -ae (f) : supply; plenty; in plural = 'troops'

cornu, -us (n) : wing (of an army); horn

corpus, -oris (n) : body

cotidianus, -a, -um : daily

cupiditas, -atis (f) : desire

decerno, -cernere, -crevi, -cretum : decide, resolve

deficio, -ficere, -feci, -fectum : be deficient, fail

differo, -ferre, distuli, dilatum : differ; spread, scatter; delay

disciplina, -ae (f) : discipline; instruction; learning

disco, -ere, didici : learn

disto, -stare : stand apart, be separate or distant

druides, -um (m pl) : druids

dum : while (with indicative); until (usually with subjunctive); provided that (with subjunctive)

educo, -ducere, -duxi, -ductum : lead out; raise up; educate

efficio, -ficere, -feci, -fectum : produce, bring about, achieve

eo : there, to that place

eques, -itis (m) : cavalryman, horseman, knight

etiam : even; also

excedo, -cedere, -cessi, -cessum : go away, depart; exceed

exercitatio, -onis (f) : exercise, training

exercitus, -us (m) : army

exiguus, -a, -um : small, scanty

existimo (1) : think; estimate

expugno (1) : capture; take by storm

extremus, -a, -um : last

fas (n) (indeclinable noun) : right; divine law

fere : almost, nearly; usually, in general
figura, -ae (f) : shape, figure, form
finis, -is (m) : limit, boundary; in plural = 'territory'
finitimus, -a, -um : neighboring, adjacent; in plural = 'neighbors'
fio, fieri, factus sum : happen, come about; become, be made
flumen, -inis (n) : river
frons, frontis (f) : front; forehead
frumentum, -i (n) : grain, wheat, corn
fuga, -ae (f) : flight
genus, -eris (n) : kind, class; race; birth
gratia, -ae (f) : popularity, agreeableness; favor; thankfulness; grace
habeo, -ere, -ui, -itum : have, hold; consider
huc : here, to this place
ibi : there
illo : to that place, there
immanis, -e : huge
impero (1) : order, command (with dative); requisition, levy (with
        accusative of thing demanded, dative of source demanded from)
impetus, -us (m) : attack; force
importo (1) : import, bring in
incito (1) : rouse, urge on; put in motion
incolo, -colere, -colui : inhabit, live in; cultivate
inde : from there, from that place
inferior, -ius : lower, inferior
infero, -ferre, -tuli, inlatum : bring in; instil
inimicus, -a, -um : hostile; as noun = 'enemy'
iniuria, -ae (f) : wrong, injustice, injury
instituo, -stituere, -stitui, -stitutum : set in place; adopt; institute, begin,
        establish
institutum, -i (n) : custom
intellego, -legere, -lexi, -lectum : understand, perceive
inter : among, between (preposition with accusative)
interior, -ius : interior, inner
intermitto, -mittere, -misi, -missum : pause, interrupt; leave free
item : likewise
iter, itineris (n) : journey, march; route
iubeo, -ere, iussi, iussum : order
iugum, -i (n) : yoke, collar (on oxen etc.); ridge
ius, iuris (n) : right, justice, law
lac, lactis (n) : milk
latitudo, -inis (f) : width, breadth
latus, -a, -um : broad
latus, -eris (n) : side
legatus, -i (m) : envoy, ambassador; deputy, second-in-command
legio, -onis (f) : legion

lex, legis (f) : law
liberi, -orum (m pl) : children
libertas, -atis (f) : freedom, liberty
licet, -ere, -uit (or *licitum est*) : it is permitted (impersonal verb)
longe : by far
longitudo, -inis (f) : length
magnitudo, -inis (f) : size; greatness
maleficium, -i (n) : wrongdoing, harm, mischief
maritimus, -a, -um : of the sea, maritime
materia, -ae (f) : timber; material
maxime : very, most, especially
milia passuum : miles
modo : only, merely, just
multitudo, -inis (f) : great number, multitude
munitio, -onis (f) : fortification; building
nascor, nasci, natus sum : be born; be found
natio, -onis (f) : tribe, race, people
necessario : necessarily
non nullus, -a, -um : some, several
nullus, -a, -um : no, none
ob : because of, on account of (preposition with accusative)
obses, -idis (c) : hostage
occido, -cidere, -cidi, -cisum : kill
omnino : altogether
oppidum, -i (n) : town
opus, -eris (n) : work
orior, oriri, ortus sum : arise, rise
paene : almost
par, -is : equal, like
pars, partis (f) : part; side, direction
pateo, -ere, -ui : extend; lie open, be exposed
paulum : a little, to some extent
pecus, -oris (n) : cattle
pellis, -is (f) : skin, hide
pello, pellere, pepuli, pulsum : rout; strike; drive
periculum, -i (n) : danger
permaneo, -manere, -mansi, -mansum : remain
persuadeo, -suadere, -suasi, -suasum : persuade (with dative of person(s) persuaded)
pertineo, -tinere, -tinui : pertain, concern; extend
pervenio, -venire, -veni, -ventum : reach, arrive at
pes, pedis (m) : foot
peto, -ere, -ivi, -itum : request, entreat; seek; go after, make for
plerumque : generally
plerusque, -aque, -umque : most, the greater part

pondus, -eris (n) : weight
pons, pontis (m) : bridge
potestas, -atis (f) : power
praemium, -i (n) : reward, prize
praesto, -stare, -stiti, -stitum : be superior; show
praesum, -esse, -fui : be in charge (with dative)
praeter : except; besides; beyond (preposition with accusative)
praeterea : besides
premo, -ere, pressi, pressum : press, oppress
proelium, -i (n) : battle
proficiscor, -ficisci, -fectus sum : set out, start
prohibeo, -hibere, -hibui, -hibitum : prevent, hinder, keep from
propter : on account of (preposition with accusative)
propterea quod : because
proximus, -a, -um : nearest, next; last
pugna, -ae (f) : fight, battle
puto (1) : think, consider, judge
quisquam, quaequam, quidquam (or *quicquam*) : anyone, anything
quisque, quaeque, quidque : each, each one
quo : where, whither
quot annis : every year
ratio, -onis (f) : reason; method, theory, plan; account
recipio, -cipere, -cepi, -ceptum : take back; receive; with a reflexive
      pronoun = 'retreat'
reddo, reddere, reddidi, redditum : give back, restore; render; give in
      return
regnum, -i (n) : royal power; kingdom; supremacy
relinquo, -linquere, -liqui, -lictum : leave, abandon
reliquus, -a, -um : remaining, rest, left
reperio, reperire, repperi, repertum : find, find out, discover
revertor, -verti, -versus sum : return
septentriones, -um (m pl) : north; the seven stars of the Great Bear (or
      Little Bear) Constellation
servitus, -utis (f) : slavery, servitude
singulus, -a, -um : individual, single, one at a time
sol, -is (m) : sun
solum, -i (n) : soil; ground, bottom, floor
spatium, -i (n) : interval, time; space, distance
spes, spei (f) : hope
statuo, -ere, -ui : decide; fix, set
studeo, -ere, -ui : be eager for; study (both with dative)
sua sponte : by themselves, by their own efforts; voluntarily
superior, -ius : higher, superior; former
sustineo, -tinere, -tinui, -tentum : support, hold up; withstand, check
tantus, -a, -um : so great, so much

tardo (1) : slow down, delay
telum, -i (n) : weapon, dart, javelin
teneo, -ere, -ui, tentum : hold; maintain
tertius, -a, -um : third
totus, -a, -um : all, whole, entire
transeo, -ire, -ii (or *-ivi*), *-itum* : cross, go over
tributum, -i (n) : tax; tribute
ullus, -a, -um : any
ulterior, -ius : further
unde : from where, whence
undique : on all sides; from all sides
usus, -us (m) : use, advantage; practice; need
uterque, -traque, -trumque : each, both
utor, uti, usus sum : use
venatio, -onis (f) : hunting, hunt
vergo, -ere : lie, incline
vero : indeed, truly
versor, -ari, -atus sum : be involved in
vicus, -i (m) : village; a quarter or ward of a town
virtus, -utis (f) : bravery, courage; manliness; virtue
vis, vis (f) : force, violence; plural *vires, virium* = 'strength'
vivo, -ere, vixi, victum : live
voluntas, -atis (f) : consent; wish, will

BIBLIOGRAPHY

This list of secondary sources is limited to books, articles and reviews cited in the endnotes.

Adcock, F.E., *Caesar as a Man of Letters* (Cambridge 1956)

Badian, E., *Foreign Clientelae 264-70 B.C.* (Oxford 1958)

Badian, E., *Roman Imperialism in the Late Republic* (Ithaca, New York 1968)

Balsdon, J.P.V.D., 'The Veracity of Caesar', *Greece and Rome* (1957)

Balsdon, J.P.V.D., Reviews and Discussions, *Journal of Roman Studies* (1955)

Carrington, R.C., *Caesar - De Bello Gallico V* (Bristol 1984)

Cary, M. and Scullard, H.H., *A History of Rome* (New York 1975)

Casson, L., *The Ancient Mariners* (New York 1959)

Chadwick, N., *The Druids* (Cardiff 1966)

Cook, S.A., Adcock, F.E. and Charlesworth, M.P. (eds.), *Cambridge Ancient History*, Vol. IX (Cambridge 1932)

Cunliffe, B., *The Celtic World* (Maidenhead 1979)

Ellis, P.B., *Caesar's Invasion of Britain* (London 1978)

Fowler, P.J., *The Farming of Prehistoric Britain* (Cambridge 1983)

Frere, S., *Britannia: A History of Roman Britain* (London 1987)

Gelzer, M., *Caesar: Politician and Statesman* (Cambridge, Massachusetts 1968)

Hammond, N.G.L. and Scullard, H.H. (eds.), *Oxford Classical Dictionary* (Oxford 1978)

Handford, S.A. and Gardner, J.F., *Caesar - The Conquest of Gaul* (Harmondsworth 1982)

John, D.A.S., *Caesar's Expeditions to Britain* (Bristol 1987)

Kenney, E.J. (ed.), *Cambridge History of Classical Literature*, Vol. II (Cambridge 1982)

Laing, L., *Celtic Britain* (New York 1979)

Powell, T.G.E., *The Celts* (London 1980)

Rambaud, M., *L'Art de la Deformation Historique dans les Commentaires de Cesar* (Paris 1953)

Rice Holmes, T., *Ancient Britain and the Invasions of Julius Caesar* (Oxford 1907)

Rice Holmes, T., *Caesar's Conquest of Gaul* (Oxford 1911)

Scullard, H.H., *From the Gracchi to Nero* (London 1970)

Sherwin-White, A.N., 'Caesar as an Imperialist', *Greece and Rome* (1957)

Sherwin-White, A.N., Reviews and Notices of Publications, *Journal of Roman Studies* (1958)

Stevens, C.E., *Antiquity*, XXI (1947)

Stevens, C.E., 'The *Bellum Gallicum* as a Work of Propaganda', *Latomus*, XI (1952)

Tierney, J.J., 'The Celtic Ethnography of Posidonius', *Proceedings of the Royal Irish Academy*, Vol. 60, Sect. C, No. 5 (1960)

Walker, A.T., *Caesar's Gallic War* (Chicago 1907)

Walser, G., *Caesar und die Germanen* (Wiesbaden 1956)

Webster, G., *The Roman Invasion of Britain* (London 1980)

Wiseman, A. and P., *The Battle for Gaul* (Boston 1980)

ABOUT THE AUTHOR

John Sang holds degrees from the University of Natal, the University of Cape Town and the University of Cambridge. He taught Classics at the University of Cape Town before coming to the United States in 1981. Since 1985 he has been chairman of the Classics Department at Crossroads School for Arts and Sciences in Santa Monica, California.